LOCALS RULE

Historical Lessons for Creating Local Defense Forces for Afghanistan and Beyond

Austin Long, Stephanie Pezard, Bryce Loidolt, Todd C. Helmus

Prepared for the Special Operations Joint Task Force—Afghanistan
Approved for public release; distribution unlimited

NATIONAL DEFENSE RESEARCH INSTITUTE

The research described in this report was prepared for the Special Operations Joint Task Force–Afghanistan. The research was conducted within the RAND National Defense Research Institute, a federally funded research and development center sponsored by the Office of the Secretary of Defense, the Joint Staff, the Unified Combatant Commands, the Navy, the Marine Corps, the defense agencies, and the defense Intelligence Community under Contract W74V8H-06-C-0002.

Library of Congress Cataloging-in-Publication Data

Locals rule : historical lessons for creating local defense forces for Afghanistan and beyond / Austin Long ... [et al.].
   p. cm.
  Includes bibliographical references.
  ISBN 978-0-8330-7659-5 (pbk. : alk. paper)
  1. Counterinsurgency—Case studies. 2. Paramilitary forces—Case studies. 3. Militia–Case studies. 4. Combined operations (Military science)—Case studies. 5. Internal security—Case studies. I. Long, Austin G. II. Title: historical lessons for creating local defense forces for Afghanistan and beyond.
  U241.L63 2012
  355.3'51—dc23
                                      2012035710

The RAND Corporation is a nonprofit institution that helps improve policy and decisionmaking through research and analysis. RAND's publications do not necessarily reflect the opinions of its research clients and sponsors.

RAND® is a registered trademark.

Cover images, top left: Civilian Irregular Defense Group Program training in Vietnam (U.S. Army Center of Military History); top right: a young Harki fighter in French Algeria, circa 1961 (Jean Poussin); bottom: Afghan Local Police (U.S. Army).

Published 2012 by the RAND Corporation
1776 Main Street, P.O. Box 2138, Santa Monica, CA 90407-2138
1200 South Hayes Street, Arlington, VA 22202-5050
4570 Fifth Avenue, Suite 600, Pittsburgh, PA 15213-2665
RAND URL: http://www.rand.org/
To order RAND documents or to obtain additional information, contact
Distribution Services: Telephone: (310) 451-7002;
Fax: (310) 451-6915; Email: order@rand.org

Preface

Local defense forces have often played a key role in counterinsurgencies throughout the 20th century. Today, local defense forces in the form of the Afghan Local Police constitute a major arm of the U.S. strategy to secure Afghanistan. This book seeks to draw lessons from previous efforts to build local defense forces. Specifically, it analyzes the use and management of local defense forces in eight major counterinsurgencies, from Indochina to Operation Iraqi Freedom. The goal is to inform U.S. and allied operations in Afghanistan as well as other current or future conflicts. The book concludes that local defense forces can be highly effective in helping to defeat an insurgency but that the management of these forces presents enormous challenges. The final chapter summarizes key lessons learned and best practices for the management of local defense forces.

This research was sponsored by the Special Operations Joint Task Force–Afghanistan and conducted within the International Security and Defense Policy Center of the RAND National Defense Research Institute, a federally funded research and development center sponsored by the Office of the Secretary of Defense, the Joint Staff, the Unified Combatant Commands, the Navy, the Marine Corps, the defense agencies, and the defense Intelligence Community.

For information on RAND's International Security and Defense Policy Center, see http://www.rand.org/nsrd/ndri/centers/isdp.html or contact the director (contact information is provided on the web page).

Contents

Summary

Local defense by police or paramilitary units has been a common tactic in counterinsurgency. These forces, known under names as diverse as militias, self-defense forces, local patrols, neighborhood watch groups, or civil defense forces, represent a "bottom-up" approach to security that focuses on the community or village level, rather than national level. Counterinsurgents have traditionally relied on local defense forces for a number of reasons. These units act as a force multiplier for regular armies that must cover large swaths of territory, and they have an unmatched knowledge of the local terrain and populations. Local defense forces may also be more motivated to fight than many regulars, because they directly see the results of security improvements on their families and community. The effective employment of local defense forces also depletes the potential recruiting pool of insurgents, while providing the central government with some sense of perceived if not actual popular support.

The use of local defense forces is not, however, devoid of risks. Militias often represent parochial interests that may, if unchecked, ultimately promote lawlessness, increase insecurity, and undermine the state. They may lack the discipline and training usually expected from regular troops and they may attempt to settle scores against other local groups, leading to an escalation of violence and political fragmentation at the local level. In addition, local defense forces are not immune from corruption and so may engage in predatory behavior against their own population. Finally, the proximity with insurgents that make them a precious source of intelligence may also lead them to defect to the enemy, sometimes with the arms provided by their protectors.

Utilizing local defense forces in counterinsurgency (COIN) can be a high reward/high risk strategy, making it particularly critical to identify the factors that seem to increase or mitigate these risks—especially since this strategy appears to be as widespread today as it was in the past. With the recent development of the Afghan Local Police (ALP) as a major part of the U.S.-led counterinsurgency campaign in Afghanistan, lessons learned from earlier efforts to build local defense are needed more than ever.

This study examines eight cases of local defense forces used in the context of counterinsurgency in Indochina, Algeria, South Vietnam, Oman, El Salvador, southern Lebanon, Afghanistan, and Iraq (Chapters Two through Nine). These case studies cover an extensive time period (from 1945 to the present) and geographic scope, as well as a wide range of intervening countries and regimes, including the United States, the United Kingdom, France, Israel, and the Soviet Union. Chapter Ten highlights lessons learned from these eight cases in a comparative analysis and applies them to the current development of the ALP, in order to outline potential challenges and to suggest a way forward that takes into account the historical experience.

Historical Examples of Local Defense Forces in COIN Campaigns

Indochina. The French made extensive use of local defense forces in their war against the Vietminh in Indochina. These forces, frequently placed behind enemy lines, helped the French make up for insufficient troop numbers. They also proved highly flexible and were well adapted to a particularly harsh combat environment. Still, challenges soon became apparent. Pockets of resistance behind enemy lines (*maquis*) provided more of a long-term strategy than an expedient solution, as local defense forces had to be carefully consolidated before they could be expanded. In addition, local defense forces lost some of their effectiveness when fielded far from their community or region of origin. Finally, short-changing local defense forces in terms of salaries, benefits, and equipment for budgetary reasons undermined their morale and performance, leading in some cases to desertions with or without arms and underlining the importance of making a full commitment to local defense forces before embarking on such efforts.

Colonial Algeria. The French also attempted to employ local defense forces, known as *harkis*, against the pro-independence National Liberation Front (FLN). Not only did harkis prove valuable for patrolling and intelligence collection, they also showed high combat value as long as careful selection, good working conditions, good command, and proper training were present. The infamous fate suffered by the harkis after the war, however, and the ensuing morale crisis in the military for those officers who did not manage to save "their" harkis from FLN reprisals, highlight with particular acuity the need to plan early for the return of local defense forces to civilian life or their integration into host nation forces.

South Vietnam. The United States undertook two major efforts at setting up local defense forces: the Civilian Irregular Defense Group (CIDG) and the Combined Action Platoon (CAP) programs. The CIDG experienced difficulties early on—rapid expansion resulted in poor quality of recruits, and employing CIDG in far-off locations and in an offensive capacity proved unpopular. In addition, the transition of these units from U.S. control to the government of South Vietnam was a failure, with Saigon mismanaging the CIDG to the point of provoking grave mutinies in late 1964. The CAP was different in that it built on local defense forces that existed previously (Popular Forces, PF, and Regional Forces, RF). Under close oversight of U.S. Marines who had volunteered for this job, the PF and RF provided quality intelligence. Relations were also much more harmonious with the government of South Vietnam, which had taken part in the program from the very beginning.

Oman. In Dhofar, British forces trained and armed defense units initially made up of former insurgents. These units, named *firqat*, showed mixed performance due to varied levels of training, but their intimate knowledge of the terrain and complex social dynamics of the region proved invaluable in terms of intelligence. Firqat experienced tensions with the government of Oman but nevertheless succeeded in cooperating closely with the Omani military, into which they eventually transitioned without major incident.

El Salvador. The U.S. experience of training civil defense units was marred by challenges from the beginning. A small in-country U.S. presence led to a hands-off, "train the trainer" approach that did not provide the level of oversight that such militias required. The program had weak support from the government of El Salvador, and communities that had experienced abuses at the hands of previous militias had little incentive to support these units (at least until a new program, Municipales en Accion, mitigated this reluctance to some extent). Overall, the civil defense units proved to be of little operational use. They preyed on the population and were confined to static activities. What little intelligence they provided was poorly exploited by a central government that did not trust them.

Lebanon. From 1978 to 2000, Israel sought to counter the influence of the Palestinian Liberation Organization (PLO) and, after 1983, Hezbollah, by arming, training, and financing local defense forces in southern Lebanon. These local forces included the Free Lebanon Army (FLA), its successor, the South Lebanon Army (SLA), as well as the Home Guards. These forces originally provided Israel with a useful buffer between its northern border and South Lebanon, but they also engaged in brutal and abusive behavior. A combination of internal deficiencies (including poor representativeness of the local population and almost exclusively economic, rather than political, motivations) as well as pressure from the Lebanese government, which had not been involved in these programs, resulted in the eventual collapse of these forces when Israeli support against Hezbollah was withdrawn.

Afghanistan. The Soviet Union relied on different types of militias to quell the insurgency against its protégé, the Democratic Republic of Afghanistan. These included "ideological" militias, border militias, and regional or territorial forces. The regional forces drew heavily on their tribal and ethnic ties and were highly personalized—one example being the Uzbek militia of Abdul Rashid Dostum. Although some reached a considerable size, they played little role as counterinsurgency forces because the funds they received from the government bought their neutrality and not their loyalty. This arrangement came to an end when Soviet financial support dried out, leading to further destabilization of the country.

Iraq. The success of the Sons of Iraq (SOI) in Anbar province owes much to Al Qaeda in Iraq (AQI)'s strategic mistakes, such as seeking to extort revenue from tribal leaders. This provided the United States with tribal leaders willing to fight what had become a common enemy. In this endeavor, the U.S. Army benefitted from the Marine Corps' earlier experiences with such groups as the Hamza Brigade. The SOI were on the U.S. Army's payroll, but recruiting was left to the locals, who knew social dynamics best. The government of Iraq initially proved skeptical of the effort and the SOI and Iraqi armed forces experienced tensions, which have been ameliorated but not eliminated. Overall, the considerable gains in security achieved by U.S. forces over that time period suggest that the SOI were a tactical and strategic success in the medium term but perhaps not in the long run.

Comparative Analysis and Lessons Learned

Although these cases differ widely in terms of their time frame, geographic location, and the countries that intervened, they offer a number of strikingly similar lessons, suggesting that these past experiences can usefully inform current and future efforts.

The first lesson is that politics is paramount in local defense operations. The United States, when seeking to support local defense, must assiduously manage a trilateral relationship between itself, the host nation government, and the local actors it wants to incorporate into local defense forces. There is frequently friction in these relationships; if not carefully managed, this friction can make the local defense effort ineffective. Of particular importance is the role of U.S. oversight of local defenders in mitigating friction and a measured pace of expansion of these programs. Rapid expansion can greatly increase friction when oversight is strained. Finding the proper balance between speed of expansion and proper oversight is one of the central challenges of these programs and requires careful case-by-case assessment.

Second, the real value of local defense forces lies in intelligence rather than manpower or combat ability. The synergy between U.S. combat capability and local defender intelligence is devastating to insurgents, who face a choice between being defeated piecemeal by local defense forces that can identify them or massing to confront local defenders, which then makes them vulnerable to U.S. firepower. However, misuse of local defense forces as semi-conventional offensive forces can greatly reduce their effectiveness.

Third, local history can limit the effectiveness of local defense. Where government-affiliated paramilitaries have existed before, locals may be highly skeptical of them if the behavior of these units was negative. Similarly, insurgent behavior can positively affect efforts to build local defense forces if such behavior antagonizes the local population.

Fourth, efforts to build local defense often require more than U.S. military support. Both the Central Intelligence Agency (CIA) and the U.S. Agency for International Development (USAID) have provided effective, sometimes critical, support to local defense. CIA and USAID have unique authorities and/or skill sets for managing the often fractious politics and economics of local defense. Integrating these agencies into future programs will likely be crucial to success.

Fifth, relationships should be maintained with the conventional military forces that actually secure and hold terrain. Units assigned to support local defense forces need flexibility and autonomy, particularly in terms of logistics, but they also need support and good relations with conventional forces. Flexibility and autonomy are needed in order to tailor support for local defense to the unique local conditions. The support of conventional forces—and indeed security force coordination generally—is crucial to ensuring that the intelligence gathered by local defense forces is properly exploited and that local defenders are protected from a massed enemy.

Sixth, it is important to avoid insurgent strongholds when building local defense forces. Local defense forces should be built in areas where the insurgency has been weakened either by military action or insurgent defections.

Seventh, the transition of local defense forces into the formal government security apparatus or demobilization must be made with great care. In essence, making the transition correctly takes a significant amount of time, while it can be done wrong overnight. History shows that successful cases of transition take considerably longer than was anticipated and face numerous challenges.

Applying the Lessons to Afghanistan

Because the United States is supporting the development of the ALP, applying these lessons is of paramount importance, especially since Afghanistan has a long and troubled history of militias. As a result, special operations forces have made strenuous (if not always successful) efforts to dissociate the ALP from militias. The ALP are subject to all the same restrictions as the Afghan National Police, including the use of force, and are subject to extensive control and oversight.

Efforts have also been made to manage the relationship between the ALP, the Afghan government, and the United States. By transforming the Local Defense Initiative into village stability operations and the ALP, U.S. special operations forces have substantially mitigated (though not eliminated) central government concerns about the program. Ongoing high-level engagements between U.S. and Afghan leaders have kept the program on track even as the numbers of the ALP have rapidly expanded. In terms of appropriate tactical employment of the ALP, U.S. special operations forces seem to be following the lessons learned. While the ALP are frequently used for checkpoint security, this is often combined with patrolling and intelligence collection.

Concerns exist, however, that rapid expansion could begin to weaken the current relative harmony between U.S. special operations forces, local actors, and the Afghan government. Finally, the nature of post-conflict transformation and/or demobilization of the ALP is an open question. Although the program is still recent, the historical cases suggest that a slow demobilization or transformation into a permanent police auxiliary, like the firqat, would be best for Afghan stability.

SOI   Sons of Iraq

TAA   Arabic acronym for Anbar Revolutionaries

USAID   U.S. Agency for International Development

UT   Territorial Units

WAD   *Wizarat-e Amaniyyat-e Dawlati* (Afghan Ministry for State Security)

CHAPTER ONE

Introduction

The importance of providing security for the population has been accepted as the sine qua non of a school of counterinsurgency known as the "hearts and minds" approach. This approach argues that by securing the population, counterinsurgents drain the sea (or swamp) that insurgents lurk within, cutting them off from recruits, resources, and intelligence. The insurgents will then be condemned to wither away in unpopulated hinterlands.[1]

But securing the population is no small matter. It requires the persistent presence of security forces (police, military, or paramilitary) capable of excluding insurgents from the population. This can require large numbers of these forces to be tied down at a potentially considerable cost.

This, in turn, leads to the observation that allowing (or requiring) the population to secure itself may be the most efficient means to cut off the insurgents from the people. It is therefore no surprise that many counterinsurgencies feature the use of some form of "self-defense force," typically a paramilitary or auxiliary police, in rural villages or urban neighborhoods. These forces, drawn from the community, often have a deep understanding of the social networks and local grudges that animate an insurgency, giving them a substantial intelligence advantage over other types of security forces.[2] Indeed, in some cases

---

[1] For discussion of the evolution of the schools of counterinsurgency theory, see Shafer, 1988; Marquis, 2000; and Long, 2006.

[2] Lyall, 2010. See also Petersen, 2001.

they are former insurgents or have family in the insurgency, giving them unmatched insight into insurgent operations. Furthermore, they are often part-time and their salaries are relatively inexpensive. Finally, because they are fighting at home, these forces can potentially be among the most motivated of security forces.

Combined, these advantages ensure that local self-defense forces can limit all but the most determined insurgent efforts to reestablish contact with a given village or neighborhood. Yet despite this potential, these programs have a mixed track record in counterinsurgency. Sometimes they become little more than "death squads," or parasitic militia preying on the population. Other times they simply fail to provide security, squandering counterinsurgency resources. At worst, they provide resources, such as arms, to the insurgency as would-be village defenders sell or give arms to their erstwhile enemies.

The current counterinsurgency in Afghanistan has been marked by several efforts to create such local defense forces. The most recent, currently called the Afghan Local Police (ALP) program is one of the main pillars of the current counterinsurgency strategy of the International Security Assistance Force (ISAF).[3] This program, which uses U.S. forces (principally special operations forces) to train village self-defense forces, has shown substantial potential but has also generated significant concern about the potential to create militia forces that could in the long run be more destabilizing than helpful.

This book has two principal purposes. The first is to distill lessons learned from historical attempts to build local defense forces. It examines efforts by the United States, Britain, France, the Soviet Union, and Israel to generate these forces. These cases are South Vietnam, El Salvador, Iraq, Oman, southern Lebanon, Indochina, Afghanistan, and Algeria.

For purposes of case selection, we define a local defense force as a paramilitary formation drawn from a particular geographic subunit of a state (village, district, province, etc.) and focused on providing security against an insurgent force in that subunit. In some cases, there is

---

3   See, for example, the discussion by ISAF commander Gen. John Allen in Scarborough, 2012.

an ethnic or religious element to local defense but this is not a requirement for our definition. Note, too, that some local defense forces over
time shift away from local defense missions. We include these units in
our studies but indicate this change of mission and its consequences.

Our case selection focused on efforts to build local defense forces
by countries supporting counterinsurgency efforts in other countries
(acting as a "third-party" counterinsurgent). While the resulting lessons may not be universally applicable, they should nevertheless be
useful for any third-party counterinsurgent, an important subset of
counterinsurgency. Note that the French counterinsurgency in Algeria
was, from the perspective of the French, conducted on French soil.

The second purpose is to examine the ALP program based on primary and secondary sources, along with author fieldwork in Afghanistan in 2010 and 2011. We then apply insights from the historical cases
to the ALP. This should not only provide a check on the findings from
historical cases but also give additional insight into the dynamics of
local defense forces generally.

qualities" as well as their "loyalty," to which two guarantors had to testify at the time of the auxiliary's recruitment.[15]

The use of these auxiliaries was closely regulated. A July 1949 note from the French forces command in southern Vietnam noted that auxiliaries should not be used as messengers, gardeners, cooks, waiters, cleaners, or in any other task unrelated to combat or surveillance. They were not supposed to be used in regular units, either, whether to replace soldiers or to bring reinforcement to an undermanned unit.[16] Rather, the purpose of auxiliaries was to take advantage of their knowledge of local conditions in defense or combat positions. They had no formal contracts (the 1948 Partisan Status mentions a "moral contract") and could be dismissed at any time.[17]

Auxiliaries belonged to many different categories. Some were unarmed, but most carried weapons and worked as guards or belonged to self-defense groups, religious militias, Military Auxiliary Companies (*compagnies de supplétifs militaires*, or CSM), or commandos. These categories often overlapped. Religious militias largely played a self-defense role, while some self-defense units fulfilled the same tasks as the CSM,[18] and selected members of the CSM could be integrated into the commandos.

Unarmed auxiliaries were divided between "first category" auxiliaries, which included guides and interpreters, and a "second category" encompassing manual laborers and porters.[19] They received a salary but, unlike some armed auxiliaries, they did not receive

---

[15] *Instruction provisoire sur le statut du partisan indochinois*, 1948.

[16] De Latour, 1949.

[17] After 1952, auxiliaries who had been taught how to drive were given a one-year contract to ensure that they would remain in the army and not look for (better paid) employment as civilian drivers (de Linares, 1952).

[18] See, for instance, Barboteu, 1952.

[19] Bodin, 2004, p. 40. Auxiliaries were almost exclusively men, although a small number of Vietnamese women were hired as nurses (Bodin, 2004, p. 51). The difficulty of infiltrating male agents in Vietminh-controlled territory led to the set-up of an operation code-named "mission Tomate" that recruited and trained six young women to gather intelligence behind enemy lines (Fournier, 1953).

food or clothing.[20] The French preferred locals for such tasks because of the ease of such recruitment and these recruits' knowledge of the local environment—particularly important for guides and porters. Interpreters were chosen preferably from among European and Indochinese locals to keep CEFEO's requests to Paris to a minimum.[21]

Most auxiliaries, however, were armed. A large number of them were confined to static defense roles, guarding critical infrastructure and military positions. Railway Guards (*Gardes voies ferrées*, or GVF) patrolled along railways, removed mines, and protected repair teams while they worked on the tracks. This was a high-risk job, as railways were a prime target for the Vietminh. GVF received a salary, additional financial compensations, and the equivalent of military ranks. Their status was so similar to the CSM that they were sometimes counted with them. As of mid-January 1954, there were 4,005 GVF.[22] Another group of guards protected properties and mines; those defending plantations were known as Plantation Guards. They constituted private groups authorized by the military. Companies or plantation owners would recruit and pay their guards, but the French military armed them and could also provide them with a commander (often a *gendarme*).[23]

Ethnic minorities and religious groups hostile to the Vietminh represented another category of armed auxiliaries. This hostility stemmed from historical or cultural tensions with the Vietnamese[24] or from the exactions carried out by the (atheist) Vietminh against their popula-

---

[20] Bodin, 2004, p. 40.

[21] The number of interpreters was 989 in early 1952 and always was less than the 1,000–1,100 requested by the French Command (Bodin, 1996, pp. 65 and 67).

[22] Bodin, 1996, p. 68. Initially considered civilian auxiliaries, they were transferred to military authority in 1952 (Dulac, 1952).

[23] Bodin, 1996, p. 76; Gérin-Roze, 2000, p. 140. A 1949 letter from the plantation owners union to the French military command in southern Vietnam underlined the necessity of keeping the pay of such guards low enough to ensure that plantation workers, whose numbers were already insufficient, would not leave en masse to become guards (Letter, September 23, 1949).

[24] Also known as Annamites, from the Annam province in central Indochina.

Annamites, and were recruited in areas where the Vietminh propaganda was either not yet dominant or had failed to rally the population.[40]

Beyond guards, ethnic or religious militias, and self-defense groups, the most common type of armed auxiliaries was the CSM. Some of these companies followed regular units (*"supplétifs à la suite"*), bringing them both some degree of flexibility and a deeper knowledge of the local terrain and populations.[41] The CSM were recruited, paid, armed, and employed by the military.[42] After 1951–52, every operation undertaken in south Vietnam included one or more of these units.[43] These auxiliaries fulfilled many different roles, including reconnaissance, intelligence, making contacts with the local population, protecting convoys, and participating in offensive operations.[44]

Another category of military auxiliaries played a more static role, that of securing French surveillance towers and posts against the Vietminh.[45] The towers, established roughly a kilometer apart, had been built by the French starting in 1948, first in south Vietnam, then in the central Annam region. Posts, too, were often under the guard of auxiliaries, in order to free regular troops for more mobile and offensive tasks. The auxiliaries defended key landmarks, such as bridges or crossroads, and were also tasked with patrolling the neighboring area in teams that could range from 10 to 50 men.[46] The many posts that were manned exclusively by auxiliaries were usually located not too far from a bigger post manned by French troops. Both towers and posts were regular targets of Vietminh attacks and were vulnerable infrastructures: As of 1953, it was estimated that only about 10 percent

---

[40] Bodin, 1996, p. 77.

[41] Bodin, 2004, p. 263.

[42] Morel, 1949.

[43] Gérin-Roze, 2000, p. 140.

[44] Bodin, 2004, p. 264.

[45] After 1949, the military took over from civilian authorities for the payment of these guards (de Latour, 1949).

[46] Bodin, 1996, p. 96.

of them were built solidly enough to be capable of withstanding serious attacks.[47]

Special Purpose Auxiliaries

Commando units, too, made an extensive use of auxiliaries. Their mission was to infiltrate areas controlled by the Vietminh to ambush enemy units, destroy supplies, and collect intelligence. They were better armed and equipped than other auxiliaries. The shortage of French commanders resulted in a gradual increase in the number of auxiliaries leading commando units; French commanders would oversee groups of several commandos.

Overall, in south Vietnam, 68 out of 90 commandos belonging to either the French or Vietnamese armies were under Vietnamese or Cambodian command.[48] Indigenous commandos were ethnically homogenous (e.g., Hoa Hao commandos, Thai commandos) and, in some cases, comprised former Vietminh combatants.[49] Several hundred auxiliaries were also attached to the army's assault naval divisions (*divisions navales d'assaut* or DINASSAUT), which provided artillery support to Army units and performed maritime interdiction, surveillance, resupply, troop transport, and evacuation.[50]

A very distinct type of commando was the Composite Airborne Commando Groups (*Groupement de commandos mixtes aéroportés*, GCMA), created by General de Lattre de Tassigny in April 1951. Its name was changed to Composite Intervention Groups (*Groupement*

---

[47] Tourret, 2000, p. 175; Cassidy (2006, p. 52) notes that "the French tended to misuse these indigenous forces, particularly the auxiliaries, by positioning them and their families in isolated outposts with the hope that they would fight relentlessly to defend them. This 'war of the posts' was extremely tedious. . . . The proliferation of posts, moreover, made these forces increasingly vulnerable to attack because of the smaller size of their contingents and because their Viet Minh opponents adapted their tactics and their weaponry faster than the French-controlled forces could adapt their defensive measures."

[48] Gérin-Roze, 2000, pp. 140–141.

[49] Bodin, 2004, p. 69.

[50] Bodin, 2004, pp. 82 and 264.

Mixte d'Intervention, GMI) in December 1953. Unlike "regular" commandos, which belonged to the army, the GCMA was placed under the authority of the French intelligence service, the *Service de documentation extérieure et de contre-espionnage* (SDECE).[51] The GCMA was the operational unit (*Service Action*) of the SDECE in Indochina and had two main purposes. The first one was to harass Vietminh units through guerrilla warfare and sabotage. The GCMA's missions included ambushing small Vietminh units, attacking their camps, sabotaging their communication lines, conducting reconnaissance for other French units, and, in some cases, facilitating the evacuation of French posts by covering retreating units. Its second purpose was to counter the Vietminh's propaganda and influence the population through psychological operations and more generally by "winning" locals ideologically.[52]

The creation of the GCMA benefitted from the experience of men who had been involved in the French Resistance during World War II either in the Central Bureau of Intelligence and Operations (General Charles de Gaulle's secret services, known under its French acronym BCRA) or the "Jedburgh" teams that gathered agents from different Allied secret services and conducted sabotage operations and air drops of weapons and ammunition.[53] Another inspiration for the GCMA was the work done during World War II by the India-based *Service Action* of the French intelligence services, which carried out guerrilla operations against Japanese troops in the northern part of Indochina with the support of pro-French Montagnards.[54] The United States strongly encouraged the GCMA initiative and provided funds for it.[55]

The GCMA was organized along five regional representations (RR), each of which had one or more subordinate units called

---

[51] David, 2002, p. 49. The GCMA, however, had a particularly complex chain of command, since it was part of the SDECE but took its orders from the Joint Staff (David, 2002, p. 69).

[52] David, 2002, pp. 50, 69, and 163; Pottier, 2005, p. 126; Bodin, 2004, pp. 69, 170, and 203.

[53] David, 2002, pp. 51–53; note 39, pp. 51–52.

[54] David, 2002, pp. 53–57.

[55] David, 2002, p. 65.

antennas.[56] First, GCMA Commander Lieutenant-Colonel Edmond Grall established the typical composition of an antenna as one officer, four NCOs, one radio-operator, and a hundred local auxiliaries (hence the name *centaine* —meaning "hundred"—which was also given to antennas).[57] In reality, antennas often reached 400 men, and some had up to 1,000 men.[58] GCMA officers and NCOs came from paratrooper units, an organic link reflected in the name of the organization ("Airborne").[59] GCMA officers were recruited based on their "taste for danger, initiative and sense of responsibilities, and good knowledge of the country."[60] Because of that last requirement, only personnel with more than one tour in Indochina could be considered for these positions. Officers with experience in the French Resistance were also particularly sought after.[61]

The main purpose of the GCMA was to establish *maquis* (the same name that was used by the French Resistance during World War II), defined as pockets of resistance near or behind enemy lines from where guerrilla action (ambushes, sabotage, attacks of posts) could be carried out. The initial steps to set up a *maquis* would be to parachute trained French or Indochinese personnel above areas where a local guerrilla uprising was believed to take place (or could be initiated) and that the Vietminh had made inaccessible by land; these individuals would then establish a connection with local guerrilla leaders and secure an area for more air drops of radios, basic equipment, arms, and ammunition.[62]

The *maquis* were characterized by their mobility (they generally stayed away from villages for security reasons and lived as much as

---

[56] Pottier, 2005, p. 129.

[57] Pottier, 2005, pp. 129–130. The author notes that "This organization, which is consistent with the idea of gnawing at the Vietminh influence, was clearly a copy of the Vietminh one."

[58] Pottier, 2005, pp. 129–130.

[59] Fleury, 1994, p. 473.

[60] Navarre, 1953, author's translation.

[61] Navarre, 1953.

[62] Muelle, 1993, p. 51.

possible in the forest) and the frequency of the ambushes they lead against the Vietminh. These ambushes allowed them to release some French prisoners in transit, capture supplies, and destroy Vietminh camps and depots. Local civilians were often sent ahead of the *maquis* column to gather intelligence and facilitate the attack. *Maquis* were resupplied by air, a complicated operation whose success depended on the availability of planes, the proximity of airfields, and favorable weather.[63] According to Major Roger Trinquier, who succeeded Grall in 1953, the GCMA required one ton of material for ten men per month for its operations.[64] This logistical support was all the more critical because the *maquis* did not live off the local population—rather, the GCMA provided supplies to the local partisans and their families.[65] In order to gain or keep the loyalty of the local population, the *maquis* would provide them to the extent possible with food, goods, and medical care.[66] Indochinese staff were used in all posts of the *maquis*, including as radio operators.[67] Some Montagnards were trained in parachute jumping, use of explosives, intelligence and psychological action, and as commandos. Each RR had its own regional training center, but the GCMA could also use two larger instruction centers (Ty Wan near Saigon and Cu Dong in Tonkin).[68] As of late July 1954, the GCMA was employing 15,113 armed auxiliaries, the great majority of them in *maquis* located in northern Vietnam and Laos.[69]

---

[63] David, 2002, pp. 330, 333, and 336.

[64] Dalloz, 2006, p. 101.

[65] David, 2002, p. 336.

[66] Teulières, 1985, p. 163, quoting Trinquier.

[67] David, 2002, p. 322.

[68] Pottier, 2005, p. 139; David, 2002, p. 66. David (2002, p. 325) notes that it was mostly GCMA-employed Europeans and Annamites who initially benefited from this training; after mid-1952, the training was opened more generally to ethnic minorities from northern regions.

[69] *"Activité du groupement mixte d'intervention, 3e trimestre 1954."*

Auxiliaries and the End of the French War

After Dien Bien Phu and the Geneva Accords of July 1954, auxiliaries were offered the choice of joining the Vietnamese military or returning to civilian life. A few could also join the French military.[70] The number of CSM was reduced—first to 35 on October 1, then to 10 on November 1, and finally to zero on December 1, 1954.[71] As for the GCMA *maquis*, their existence was kept secret during the peace negotiations. The French decided to evacuate their own commanders and leave all weapons to the local populations to allow them to pursue the fighting. This decision was based on the expectation that mentioning the *maquis* would have led to their inclusion in the negotiations, and that many (if not all) of them would have, as a result, been demilitarized. Not mentioning them meant turning the *maquis* into sleeper cells that could possibly be reactivated in the future.[72] In the weeks that preceded the Geneva Accords, airdrops increased to provide the *maquis* and local population with large amounts of equipment, weapons, and ammunition while it was still allowed. A number of local leaders who had strongly and publicly supported the French were offered resettlement in the Delta region to protect them from Vietminh reprisals, but few chose to leave their communities.[73] In Laos, the *maquis* were gathered in a single organization (*Groupement de commandos parachutistes lao*) and used by the Laotian government against incursions by the local communist rebel organizations (the Pathet Lao and Vietminh).[74]

Overall, an estimated 3,500 members of *maquis* were killed or wounded during the war.[75] One historian estimates that more than one million civilians, some of them former partisans, were killed by the Vietminh as retaliation in areas formally controlled by the French, but

---

[70] Ely, 1954.

[71] Cogny, 1954.

[72] David, 2002, p. 358.

[73] David, 2002, p. 362.

[74] David, 2002, p. 365.

[75] Bodin, 2004, p. 170.

this figure is impossible to confirm.[76] It is certain, however, that many members of ethnic and religious minorities were massacred by the Vietminh once it gained control of these areas—both because of these minorities' support for the French and their resistance to Vietminh influence. In September 1954, the GMI (formerly the GCMA) was dissolved and its personnel integrated into a more classic *Service Action* of the SDECE.[77] Some French cadres had developed such strong relationships with their men in the *maquis* that ". . . they decided to stay in the mountains to keep on fighting with the tribesmen at the end of the war. The others came back to France with a deep sense of guilt."[78] The *maquis* continued the fighting with the weapons left behind by the French, and, although the Vietminh eventually eradicated all of them, it took it nearly five years to do so.[79]

Motivations for Using Auxiliaries

The French had many reasons to resort to the local recruitment pool to sustain their war effort. One reason was propaganda: If French and Indochinese were seen fighting side by side, the nationalist and anti-colonial message of the Vietminh would be undermined. Recruited Indochinese were also removed from the risk of Vietminh contagion and the Vietminh's own recruitment pool.[80] The French were also training men who could later integrate the national armies of Vietnam, Laos, and Cambodia.[81] Finally, auxiliary units were cheaper than Indochinese or European regular units:

---

[76] Brett, 1998, p. 7.

[77] David, 2002, pp. 363 and 357.

[78] Pottier, 2005, p. 142.

[79] David, 2002, p. 364; Pottier, 2005, pp. 144–145.

[80] Bodin, 2004, pp. 73, 74, and 179.

[81] These armies were largely funded by the United States (Teulières, 1985, p. 165).

Each member was paid 250 piastres per month, while an Indochinese regular would get 410 piastres and a European regular, 586.[82]

The use of local defense forces was also critical because of the constant French shortage of men during the war. General Jacques Philippe Leclerc estimated in 1946 that it would take 500,000 men to pacify Indochina and eliminate the Vietminh.[83] However, political pressure on the home front constantly kept deployed troops to a limited level and, as Taber (2002) notes,

> In August 1950, the French government actually ordered a *reduction* of the French forces in Indochina by 9,000 troops, ignoring the military realities of the situation there entirely; and the National Assembly, yielding to popular anti-war sentiment at home, required assurance that no military conscripts would be used in Indochina. In other words, it was to be a police action carried out by professionals, principally Foreign Legion, Moroccan, and other non-French troops.[84]

As a result, there were still only 200,000 French troops in late 1951. Indochinese represented one-third of the CEFEO while another third was French and the last third was made of Legionnaires, North African troops, and Sub-Saharan African troops.[85]

Last, the local population's knowledge of the terrain was extremely valuable, especially because French military personnel experienced difficulties progressing through the mountains and forests of northern Vietnam. Auxiliaries were highly resistant to the local climate. They were also extremely flexible soldiers, and the French appreciated their ability to blend into both the natural environment and the local population, particularly for commando-type operations.[86] For this reason, the French also made an extensive use of military prisoners (*prisonniers*

---

[82] Gérin-Roze, 2000, p. 140.

[83] Teulières, 1985, p. 165.

[84] Taber, 2002, p. 65. Our emphasis.

[85] Teulières, 1985, p. 165.

[86] Gérin-Roze, 2000, p. 137; Bodin, 1996, p. 73.

et internés militaires, PIM) who were irregular combatants captured fighting alongside the Vietminh.[87] They were recruited after a military investigation[88] and sent to French units to build or repair communication lines and fortifications, work as porters, and even, in some instances, join commandos (e.g., the commandos Vandenbergh and Rusconi).[89] The PIM's knowledge of Vietminh methods and tactics made them particularly valuable to the French Command.[90]

Assessment

Commanding officers vary widely in their assessment of the efficiency of auxiliary forces.[91] A 1954 note from the commander of the French forces in northern Vietnam underlined their advantages: They were light (due to the lack of heavy weapons and to carrying a smaller pack), knew villages and populations, could move on local terrain and maneuver well on it, could speak the local language, and knew the Vietminh and its methods well.[92] Bodin (2004) notes that auxiliary companies were excellent for search and reconnaissance.[93] Expectations also differed according to the type of group considered: Self-defense groups were lightly armed and barely trained, while some commandos were seasoned fighters.[94] Religious minorities generally proved solid allies, at

---

[87] Regular Vietminh combatants belonged to the Prisoners of War category.

[88] Cogny, 1953.

[89] Bodin, 1996, p. 64; Bodin, 2004, p. 41. Both commandos experienced outstanding successes but were brought to a premature end because of treason within their ranks. Vandenbergh was killed in his sleep by one of his men in January 1952; Rusconi was killed during a night attack of the Vietminh against his commando's base one month later.

[90] Bodin, 1996, p. 64.

[91] Gérin-Roze, 2000, pp. 143–144.

[92] Cogny, 1954.

[93] Bodin, 2004, pp. 263–264.

[94] Bodin, 2004, p. 265.

least when their interests aligned with those of the French military.[95] The benefits of using auxiliaries were clear enough for the French Command to hire 10,300 additional auxiliaries in 1950 only.[96]

Some groups could prove unstable, however, reducing their ability to provide effective assistance to the French. The Caodaists experienced internal crises as well as severe disagreements with the French regarding the extent of the territory that would fall under their control in exchange for their support.[97] The Hoa Hao, too, could prove unpredictable; between 1948 and 1951, they were deeply absorbed by their own internal struggles for power and committed acts of banditry against civilians, as well as several attacks against French forces.[98] Another issue was the fact that the Montagnard people's hatred of Annamites was sometimes superseded by their own internal rivalries; as a result, "distrust between the groups proved to be a major limitation in the conduct of operations."[99] A 1949 note from the Auxiliaries Forces Inspection noted the "lack of military and moral value of some commanders and soldiers in auxiliary units," an issue they attributed to poor selection.[100] Another note dated 1953 warns of Vietminh intentions to infiltrate auxiliary forces.[101] It is, however, difficult to assess whether auxiliary units generally proved loyal or not—especially since "desertion" figures include auxiliaries who were working without a contract and simply went back to their village.

One key factor of efficiency was keeping auxiliaries close to their region of origin. The French Command was so aware of this element

---

[95] Bodin, 1996, p. 97.

[96] Fray, 1949.

[97] Bodin, 1996, p. 97.

[98] Bodin, 1996, p. 97.

[99] Pottier, 2005, p. 142.

[100] Forces franco-vietnamiennes du sud, 1949.

[101] de Linares, 1953.

that it was integrated into its rules on how to employ auxiliaries.[102] A 1951 note called attention to the fact that auxiliaries tended to leave their units in large numbers when operations took them far from their village or region of origin. They also sometimes changed units to join one more geographically convenient for them.[103] GCMA *maquis* experienced similar issues, made all the more critical by the fact that the leadership there was often too thin to enforce credible sanctions. One author mentions an instance in which the local *maquis* leader could not keep his Meo partisans who had decided to go back to their village to celebrate the Meo New Year—leaving the *maquis* dangerously exposed to Vietminh attacks.[104] Keeping auxiliaries nearby their communities could also limit the risks of them committing exactions against the local population. A 1946 report signaling such exactions (both from Cambodians and Annamite partisans) in the Chaudoc and Travinh regions notes, "This is a general phenomenon due to the fact that partisans, because they operate far from their village and even sometimes their province of origin, escape the moral constraints of their family and community and potential sanctions by their notables."[105]

Other important factors influencing the efficiency of auxiliaries included recruitment quality, leadership, armament, and morale.[106] Insufficient leadership remained a constant issue during the war. The target figures of two officers, six NCOs, and two soldiers for 100 auxiliaries were rarely reached.[107] One author points to instances in 1948 in Tonkin in which three NCOs were commanding 200 auxiliaries; in other instances, a captain was found leading several hundred aux-

---

[102] General René Cogny wrote on July 19, 1953: "As a reminder . . . candidates for auxiliary positions must: . . . (c) Be recruited (and employed) in their province of origin" (author's translation). General Cogny reiterates here the stipulations of the 1948 Partisan Status.

[103] de Linares, 1951.

[104] David, 2002, p. 343.

[105] Letter, "Le Conseiller politique du gouvernement fédéral à monsieur le Général Commandant supérieur des T.F.E.O.," 1946. Author's translation.

[106] Bodin, 2004, p. 265.

[107] Bodin, 1996, p. 90.

iliaries, and some commandos were led by sergeants.[108] Finding a sufficient number of leaders was particularly difficult for *maquis*, whose officers and NCOs suffered from psychological isolation; these personnel were subject to intense stress, extremely difficult living conditions, the constant fear of being wounded with little hope of medical evacuation, and in some cases a feeling of paranoia that their men would turn on them.[109]

Another factor affecting morale was the fact that auxiliaries often lacked equipment and, in some instances, food.[110] Several reports underline the difficulty of keeping auxiliaries in their units in the face of low salaries, poor clothing, and generally few benefits.[111] This issue was compounded by the fact that there were different levels of payments for partisans, and that they did not receive the same amount of money or material advantages as regulars in the *maquis*, creating some tensions and, in some cases, desertions.[112] A report on the desertion of an entire auxiliary unit in 1948 highlighted "the too great difference of treatment that exists between regulars and partisans," in an area where "partisans and regulars do exactly the same work."[113] Another report lamented the tendencies to use auxiliaries to compensate for the insufficient numbers of regulars in the military—by 1953, auxiliaries were used more and

---

[108] Bodin, 1996, p. 90. General Jean de Lattre de Tassigny, upon his arrival in Indochina, dubbed the Indochinese conflict "a war of lieutenants and captains" (Muelle, 1993, p. 45).

[109] Pottier, 2005, p. 141. This author notes that "At the beginning, each centaine was theoretically commanded by an officer assisted by four NCOs [noncommissioned officers]. After Trinquier took command of the GCMA, however, French officers and NCOs were usually alone or with no more than one or two other Frenchmen per maquis band."

[110] Margueron, 1946.

[111] See, for instance, Redon, 1949.

[112] David, 2002, p. 346. This author notes that offering promotions to partisans, either within the maquis or with promises of a job in the regular army, acted as powerful motivators. However, the number of partisans who could become regulars was limited. Some efforts were made after 1953 to bridge the salary gap between partisans and regulars (David, 2002, pp. 345–346), but the salary for a French sergeant was still more than ten times the salary of an auxiliary sergeant (Brett, 1998, p. 7).

[113] "Rapport du Lt-Colonel Carbonel, 1948," Author's translation.

farther away or in environments they were unfamiliar with. Remaining in nearby villages was also a way for partisans to check on their families, as they constantly worried about potential retaliation on the part of the Vietminh.[130] This fear of retaliation led many villages to provide information and support to both the French and the Vietminh. It was also a constant strain on the morale of auxiliaries working for the GCMA, who knew that the French could not protect their families.[131]

A last challenge in employing auxiliaries, which was confined to the case of the Meo tribesmen, related to opium. The Meos cultivated 80 percent of the opium produced in Indochina at the time, and these harvests represented one of their main sources of wealth.[132] The Vietminh, too, had long been using opium as a source of funding. By 1948, it was successfully controlling 80 percent of the opium production in the Tonkin region and was aggressively promoting poppy culture in areas under its control.[133] Because of their alliance with the Meos, the French had to integrate this economic factor into their strategy, and some French commanders gained Meo support by allowing the transport of opium from its area of production to Saigon, taking away a potential source of funding from the Vietminh but also triggering what soon became known in France as the "opium scandal." This scandal resulted in the eviction of General Edmond Grall as the head of the GCMA and his replacement by Roger Trinquier. It illustrates the difficulties of working with local defense forces when their interests and values do not align well with those of the political power commanding the intervention.[134]

The localized successes of the GCMA could hardly make the difference for the French in the overall conduct of the war. While the Vietminh could offer a clear political project, there was no equivalent

---

[130]David, 2002, p. 344.

[131]Pottier, 2005, p. 142.

[132]David, 2002, pp. 349–350.

[133]David, 2002, p. 351.

[134]David, 2002, pp. 352–353.

on the French side.[135] *Maquis* were also a long-term process. One author notes that "the establishment of a *maquis* had to be considered as a very long-term decision. Its establishment was already an eight-month process, and to build confidence among the population might take years. To fight insurgency in this way was clearly a long-term task; however, the results achieved also proved to be long-lasting."[136] A number of *maquis* continued the fighting even after the French had left. However, with no outside support, most of these pockets of resistance were bound to be eventually wiped out by the Vietminh.

Conclusion

The intensive use of auxiliaries in the Indochina War underlines the many benefits that the French expected from it: cheaper recruits who could make up for the lack of troops sent from France; propaganda tools against the Vietminh's nationalist arguments; experts on the local terrain, languages, and populations; and flexible soldiers who were already perfectly adapted to their environment. Setting up a self-defense force was also perceived as a way to get local populations to take their defense in their own hands.[137] The limits of the use of auxiliaries became apparent, too. *Maquis* were powerless against large conventional units,[138] and it was important to take the time to consolidate a *maquis* and properly train its partisans before expanding it.[139] As a general rule, auxiliaries had to remain close to their community or region of origin. Another key element was securing their families against Vietminh retaliation. The constant struggle of the French Command to keep in check the budget of a war unpopular in Paris also led to short-changing auxiliaries in terms of salaries, benefits, and equipment. This undermined

---

[135] David, 2000, p. 162.

[136] Pottier, 2005, pp. 144–145.

[137] Bodin, 1996, p. 96.

[138] Pottier, 2005, p. 144. The Lao Kay region *maquis*, for instance, were swept out by Chinese troops in May 1952 (Dalloz, 2006, p. 101).

[139] David, 2000, p. 163.

conscripts.[4] It is also the result of the intensive use that the French military made of local defense forces during the war.

Local defense forces were categorized in different groups with distinct purposes and legal statuses. They included Mobile Groups for Rural Protection (*Groupes mobiles de protection rurale*, GMPR), *maghzens*, self-defense groups (*Groupes d'auto-défense*, GAD), Territorial Units (*Unités territoriales*, UT), and *harkas*. By 1960, these defense forces—which were usually, but not systematically, local in their recruitment and their missions—comprised about 100,000 men (and a few women) who were providing the French military with combat, logistical, and surveillance support.[5]

This chapter examines the different local defense forces recruited by the French and the missions they were assigned in the war against the ALN, as well as their evolution over time. It also provides an assessment of the results obtained by these forces, before examining their fate after the war and concluding with the lessons learned by the French regarding the benefits and shortcomings of the use of local defense forces.

Local Defense in the Maghreb

The use of local defense forces by the French in the Maghreb was not new to this conflict. French colonial troops had long employed locally recruited men (usually known as *goums*, meaning "troops" in Arabic) as police auxiliaries.[6] In the case of Algeria, resorting to local personnel was made all the more necessary by the fact that a large number of

---

[4] This chapter focuses on local defense forces and will therefore not examine the many cases of FSNA who were part of the French army as regulars or conscripts. On FNSA conscripts in the French Army during the Algerian War, see Chauvin, 1995, pp. 21–30.

[5] This rough overall estimate is based on the following figures: 60,000 harkis in 1960–1961; 20,000 moghaznis in early 1960; 30,000 GAD in 1959–60; and up to 12,000 GMS (Hautreux, 2008, pp. 39–44).

[6] Ageron, 1995, p. 3. For a historical account of the use of local populations by the French military in its colonies, see Faivre, 1995, pp. 10–13. This author notes that shortly before the 1954 insurrection, then–General Governor of Algeria Roger Léonard had requested the

troops were still in Indochina when the insurrection struck in 1954. The French government attempted to reestablish order in Algeria by creating the GMPR in early 1955, which initially consisted of 30 units of 100 men each.[7] The purpose of the GMPR was to operate as a local police force in rural and remote areas to protect the population and property by conducting patrols, checkpoints, and searches. They also had the ability to act as backups for other security units.[8] GMPR were composed, by a large majority (75–80 percent), of FSNA and were initially put under the command of "French of European descent" (FSE) policemen.[9] Recruitment was local because successful candidates were expected to have a good knowledge of the terrain and population; it also targeted former combatants because of their military experience and knowledge of how to use a weapon.[10] In March 1958, GMPR were moved under military authority and FSE NCOs took over command from police officers. The name of these groups was changed to Mobile Security Groups (GMS), but their missions remained the same.[11] Through their law enforcement and surveillance role in the countryside, they played a key role in the "pacification" process, with their number eventually reaching 12,000.[12]

With the worsening of the violence in 1955, Algeria's General Governor Jacques Soustelle created the Specialized Administrative

---

creation of "civilian goums" who would complement the existing police forces in rural areas, but his request was denied for lack of available funds (Faivre, 2001, p. 34).

[7] Faivre, 2001, pp. 55–56.

[8] Hautreux, 2008, pp. 38–39.

[9] Hautreux, 2008, pp. 38–39.

[10] Ageron, 1995, p. 4; Faivre, 2001, p. 34 ; Hautreux, 2008, pp. 38–39. Gortzak (2009, pp. 316–317) notes that "This is not altogether surprising as the French could draw upon a large pool of Muslim veterans to fill the ranks of their auxiliary units. France had long relied upon Muslims to man some of its most illustrious career colonial army units, such as the Tirailleurs Algériens. Moreover, a large number of Algerian Muslims had served in the French forces during World War II. All in all, up to 640,000 Algerian Muslims were veterans of France's military campaign and, as such, were at least somewhat trained in military operations."

[11] Ageron, 1995, p. 5; Hautreux, 2008, p. 39.

[12] Hautreux, 2008, p. 39.

narrates the beginnings of this force in late 1954 as follows: "After noting instances where villagers in the Orléansville area had killed FLN scouts with hatchets, [French ethnologist Jean] Servier—despite considerable official opposition—had gained permission initially to create light companies from some thousand men, the able-bodied and trustworthy defectors from the FLN, or *anciens combattants*."[44] Harkis were officially recognized in 1956.[45] They operated either individually as highly mobile combatants ("*voltigeurs*"), guides, and interpreters, or in squad-sized units (*harkas*) commanded by French officers or senior NCOs.[46] The number and types of tasks they were involved in was extremely large and diverse. Some harkis were porters, cooks, hairdressers, gardeners, or mechanics. Some even took part in interrogations. Aging or wounded harkis were employed as guards.[47] Some harkis were attached to army engineer or logistics units while some were integrated into Gendarmerie brigades.[48] There were a few female harkis, the "harkettes" (up to 343 in December 1961[49]), whose main work was medical assistance and personal searches of women.[50]

Harkis were mainly recruited locally. A note on the "use of harkis" from the Army Commander in the Constantine region states that "they must know perfectly their terrain and the population, this is why they must preferably be 'locals' and it is by remaining so that they can deliver the most valuable services."[51] They consisted mostly of young rural men coming from poor backgrounds; most did not speak

---

[44] Horne, 1978, pp. 254–255.

[45] In 19th century Algeria, "harki" designated a type of military expedition; in early 20th century Morocco, it designated a police or army unit operating on a temporary basis under the command of a traditional leader (Hautreux, 2008, p. 38 citing historian Charles-Robert Ageron).

[46] Cassidy, 2006, p. 53 ; Hautreux, 2006, pp. 34 and 40.

[47] Hautreux, 2008, p. 44.

[48] Ageron, 1995, p. 6. This author estimates the number of harkis in the Gendarmerie to approximately 1,000, with 10 per brigade.

[49] Ageron, 1995, p. 6, note 4.

[50] Ageron, 1994, p. 4, note 2.

[51] Gouraud, 1960.

French, could not read or write, and had no military training.[52] There were few selection criteria to become a harki. As underlined above, good physical condition was not a prerequisite. Prospective harkis were simply subjected to a quick investigation to make sure they did not have any links with the FLN.[53] They were mostly valued for their "knowledge of the terrain, endurance, patience, and incredible observation skills."[54] A number of former FLN/ALN members (the *ralliés*, or "rallied ones") also joined the harkis.[55] Their value was mostly psychological, and *ralliés* were largely used for propaganda purposes. A May 1, 1958, instruction from Commander-in-Chief in Algeria General Raoul Salan (1956–1958) commanded the creation of "psychological teams" with nine harkis chosen preferably from among *ralliés*.[56] Rallied harkis were closely monitored, however, as they tended to desert— often with arms.[57]

Harkis were hired on a very short-term basis, directly by army commanding officers. After December 1961, they eventually received a specific legal status that included one-month, renewable contracts.[58] In spite of this short-term legal status, many harkis served for extended periods of time, as shown, for instance, by the fact that some of them obtained the equivalent of a military rank.[59] They were paid out of

---

[52] Allès, 2000, p. 142.

[53] Hautreux, 2006, p. 39.

[54] Allès, 2000, p. 143, author's translation.

[55] Hautreux (2006, p. 39) estimates their number at less than 5 percent of the total number of harkis.

[56] The mission of these teams was "to take part in the struggle against the OPA; to ensure the 'teaching' of the population; to control the organization of the population." (Letter from General Salan to the Commanding Generals of the Army Corps of Algiers, 1958.)

[57] Hautreux, 2006, p. 39. Some of these *ralliés* also became part of Captain Christian Léger's *bleus*, a network of former FLN agents who infiltrated their old units and led to the breakdown, in early 1958, of the main FLN networks in Algiers. This operation also resulted in massive internal FLN purges within Wilayas 3 and 4 (two FLN regional administrative units) that severely weakened the group (Horne, 1978, pp. 260–261).

[58] Ageron, 1995, p. 6.

[59] Hautreux, 2008, p. 42.

civilian funds, and their wages were superior to what regulars received. They lived with their families and did not receive food, or they had to pay for it.[60] They had annual leave as well as free medical care and compensation if they were wounded or became ill. Families would also get some compensation if harkis were killed in the line of duty.[61] They usually were armed with hunting rifles, but eventually about half of them received military weapons.[62]

After December 1958, some harkis were hired as *commandos de chasse* (pursuit commandos).[63] A key component of General Challe's plan to eliminate the FLN, the *commandos de chasse* were partly based on an earlier experience, started in 1958, of small commando teams that mixed FSE and FSNA.[64] The use of such commandos was also a lesson learned from the Indochina War, when the French had found that mobile and aggressive units were highly effective against guerrillas.[65] *Commandos de chasse* were elite units made up of volunteers whose numbers eventually reached 4,000 men, including 1,250 harkis.[66]

The proportion of FSNA to FSE was largely left for individual commanders to decide. A February 1959 note states that personnel should be carefully selected based on their skills "with no distinction of military unit, race or specialty" but nevertheless advised starting with a "reasonable" FSNA-to-FSE ratio before increasing the proportion of FSNA.[67] A proposal for a commando in the Sebdou subsector had 50 percent of FSE and FSNA, a proportion considered "optimal in order

---

[60] Ageron, 1994, p. 4.

[61] Ageron, 1995, p. 6.

[62] Ageron, 1994, p. 4.

[63] Ageron, 1995, p. 6.

[64] Jauffret, 2001, p. 33. On the Challe Plan see, among others, Horne, 1978, pp. 330–340; Gougeon, 2005; and Griffin, 2010.

[65] Hautreux, 2006, p. 35; Gortzak, 2009, p. 315.

[66] Xth Military Region, Constantine Army Corps, 1959. This number quickly increased: Hautreux (2008, pp. 43–44) cites 6,000 harkis in the *commandos de chasse* in mid-1960, which represents approximately 10 percent of the total number of harkis.

[67] Gambiez, 1951.

to have at the same time: a sufficient number of scouts with a good knowledge of the country, its customs, and possibly the habits of rebel groups (rallied harkis from rebel groups); a sufficient number of specialists to command the overall team and fulfill jobs that require some technical skills."[68] In yet another example, an April 1959 note established the "optimal strength" for the Marnia subsector's *commandos de chasse* at 20 percent of harkis.[69] Some *commandos de chasse* were mostly made of "*ralliés*," such as the "Commando Georges," which achieved considerable successes.[70]

The mission of these commandos was to track a given ALN unit over an extended period of time and harass it, crossing sectors if needed.[71] They could call in combat support from paratroopers and Foreign Legion units.[72] This new strategy proved extremely successful, and inflicted severe losses on the ALN.[73]

Partisan groups represent a last category of local defense forces, although they are often classified with the harkis. They consisted of communities organized around traditional leaders who had chosen to side with the French. Leaders such as Mohammed Bellounis, Belhadj Djilali (also known as Kobus), and Si Cherif received weapons from the French after 1957.[74] Taken together, these communities numbered

---

[68] Lemond, 1959, author's translation.

[69] 12th Infantry Division, 1959.

[70] Jauffret, 2001, p. 34. On the Commando Georges, see, for instance, Le Pautremat, 2004, pp. 95–103.

[71] Griffin, 2010, p. 576.

[72] Gortzak, 2009, p. 315. For a critique of the Challe plan, see Griffin, 2010, p. 578.

[73] Pimlott, 1985, pp. 66–67. Six *commandos de chasse* killed 621 ALN while sustaining only 37 killed and 56 wounded in action (Gortzak, 2009, p. 327). The same author notes that with these commandos, "The ALN units could . . . no longer easily exploit the weaknesses of the quadrillage. Neither could they simply take cover and wait for the French actions to blow over as they had in the past, moreover, as Challe's offensives were essentially of unlimited duration" (Gortzak, 2009, p. 315).

[74] Hautreux, 2006, p. 40.

a large territory and population).[87] General Salan, who had been Commander-in-Chief in Indochina in 1952–53 and led both the civilian and military authorities in Algeria after December 1956, developed a strategy known as *quadrillage*, described as "demarcating the countryside into grids, each box or quadrilateral being swept by military patrols. This method could only be implemented because Prime Minister Guy Mollet's government in Paris acceded to military demands for a major buildup of the troop levels and deployed reservists and conscripts in scores of thousands."[88] This strategy did not prove particularly successful, as ALN fighters, who knew the terrain better, could hide in the countryside and the mountains, pass as civilians, and cross back into the "boxes" that had just been cleared by the French army.[89]

Another key element of the "pacification" of Algeria was trying to gain the support of the population and denying that same support to the FLN.[90] From this perspective, the use of local forces also had a psychological purpose. It helped counter FLN propaganda by showing that FSNA supported the French side in the war. Other motivations for the French to resort to local defense forces included reducing the recruitment pool for the ALN and obtaining intelligence that locals were more likely to access because of their knowledge of the local populations.[91]

On the FSNA side, there were also multiple motivations for joining the different defense groups armed by the French. Ideology seems to have played a minimal role.[92] Ageron (1995) argues that the economic motivation dominated, as the wages were attractive for extremely

---

[87] Jauffret, 2001, p. 21.

[88] Alexander and Keiger, 2002, p. 9.

[89] Alexander and Keiger, 2002, p. 9.

[90] Hautreux, 2006, p. 36. "Pacification" included some nontraditional military tasks, such as provision of social services and education. Official documents made clear that both types of action were critical for the success of the overall "pacification" of Algeria (the word "war" was not used at the time) (see General Maurice Challe's Directive No. 1 of December 22, 1958).

[91] Hautreux, 2006, p. 34.

[92] Hautreux, 2008, p. 46.

l'ordre), which defected to the ALN three months later with 22,600 arms.[108] The Evian Accords in March had already resulted in the desertion of 6,000 military and 1,100 local forces. There were only 25,000 harkis left by April.[109]

The Evian Accords and the Fate of Local Defense Forces

A decree of March 20, 1962, offered harkis the choice between two options: joining regular army units or returning to civilian life with financial compensation for reintegration. Twenty-one thousand harkis (81.2 percent of those still in service at the time) chose the latter.[110] In April 1962, 1,134 families requested reinstallation in France, but a month later one-third of them had already changed their minds; the FLN had provided reassurances in Evian that there would be no reprisals against the harkis.[111] The French government was not particularly eager to bring harkis to metropolitan France, either, partly out of fear that they would reinforce the Organization of the Secret Army (Organisation de l'armée secrète, OAS), which gathered pro-French Algeria hardliners and had been responsible for multiple attacks in France and Algeria (including, in 1962, a failed attempt to assassinate de Gaulle).[112] As a result, in May 1962 Minister of Algerian Affairs Louis Joxe issued a telegram prohibiting individual initiatives to repatriate harkis.[113] After some attempts by the military command and Prime Minister Georges Pompidou to change this policy, a June 21, 1962, decision of

---

[108]Faivre, 1994, pp. 179–181.

[109]Faivre, 1994, p. 180.

[110]Ageron, 2000, p. 4.

[111]Ageron, 2000, pp. 4 and 6.

[112]Newspapers from both ends of the political spectrum suspected the OAS of promoting harkis' repatriation in France for that purpose. Other newspapers however denounced the abandonment of harkis (Ageron, 2000, p. 9).

[113]Ageron, 2000, p. 9.

the Algerian Affairs Committee confirmed the repatriation prohibi-
tion, with few exceptions.[114]

Meanwhile, it was rapidly becoming clear that the FLN would
not respect any of the promises it made in Evian with regards to harkis.
Organized massacres of former harkis started in mid-July all over
Algeria and, after a brief respite, started again in September.[115] In some
areas, reprisals came directly from the local population.[116] Historians
still disagree on the numbers of former local defense forces killed in
the months that followed the Evian Accords, and the fate of the harkis
has been a heated subject of debate in France ever since. One author
suggests that 50,000–75,000 French Muslims disappeared after the
cease-fire.[117] An estimate from the former Deputy Prefect of the Akbou
district, in a report to the State Council Vice-President Alexandre
Parodi in 1963, gave an estimate of 72,000 to 108,000 harkis killed.[118]
Some estimates go up to 150,000.[119]

Initially, the French government expected that 10,000 FSNA
(harkis and moghaznis) would need to be evacuated to France.[120]
Even before the cease-fire, however, some French military officers had
started organizing escape routes toward France for their harkis and
moghaznis.[121] ALN violence against those who had returned to their
villages led many families to seek refuge in French military posts,
which hosted 3,300 threatened individuals from mid-July to mid-
August 1962.[122] As exactions became more widespread in Algeria, with
harkis tortured, sent to clean minefields, mutilated, or killed with their

---

[114] Faivre, 2001, p. 59.

[115] Faivre, 1994, pp. 183 and 185.

[116] Ageron, 2000, p. 6.

[117] Faivre, 1994, p. 186.

[118] Ageron, 2000, p. 10.

[119] Ageron, 2000, p. 11.

[120] Cohen, 1980, p. 107.

[121] Monneret, 2000, p. 338.

[122] Ageron, 2000, p. 4.

entire family,[123] the number of requests for repatriation to metropolitan France exploded. Overall, between 1963 and 1970, 22,000–25,000 FSNA were rapatriated by military means; this figure does not include those who used unofficial routes to reach France.[124]

The harkis who made it to France experienced great hardship. One author notes that "Given the Harkis' lack of skills and the cultural gap between them and native Frenchmen, they could not be easily absorbed into the mainstream of French life. A large proportion was placed in camps which had served refugees during the Spanish Civil War, then refugees from Indochina. Six thousand were located in fire control and reforesting centres, and the rest in small communities, mostly in the South . . . They were not integrated into the communities in which they settled."[125] Harkis had to apply for French citizenship; the governmental grants they received for their reintegration were considerably less than what the FSE repatriated from Algeria (*Pieds Noirs*) received (70,000 francs for the former, 170,000 for the latter).[126] In Algeria, the word "harki" has become synonymous with "traitor,"[127] and it was not until December 1974 that harkis were officially recognized by France as former combatants.[128]

Assessment

An overall assessment of the combat quality of local defense forces in Algeria is extremely difficult, as situations varied widely from one harka or maghzen to the next. Some moghaznis deserted with arms, sometimes killing their SAS officer in the process; in other instances, moghaznis proved so loyal to their SAS officer that they quit en

---

[123]Horne, 1978, p. 537.

[124]Faivre, 1994, p. 186; Ageron, 2000, pp. 4–5.

[125]Cohen, 1980, pp. 108–109.

[126]Cohen, 1980, p. 108.

[127]See, for instance, Maazouzi, 2009, p. 2.

[128]Maazouzi, 2009, p. 3.

masse when that officer left or was replaced.[129] Anecdotal assessments abound—for instance, one author evokes a particularly incompetent GAD in the Sidi Bel Abbès *arrondissement* which lost five times as many people as the ALN and was particularly prone to desertions with arms[130]—but they hardly provide a reliable picture of the overall military value of these groups.

Several authors have underlined the role played by commanding officers and SAS administrators in the overall efficiency and reliability of these forces.[131] One author notes that too often, "*Harkas* were imposed on army units from above, but with little guidance to how they should be recruited, trained, and deployed. This means that they were often seen as a burden by the regular units charged with creating them. Battalion commanders had little incentive to assign their best junior commanders to command and train such units. Due to an often chronic lack of junior commanders among the regular French army units, French commanders also had little incentive to assign a large number of highly qualified officers and NCOs to these auxiliary units."[132] Another important factor affecting performance was the conditions of recruiting and deployment. Recruiting criteria were low, few officers were available to provide leadership, harkis were poorly equipped, and they received little or no training.[133] These two factors of performance are particularly salient in the case of the *commandos de chasse*: Harkis there performed extremely well because they had been chosen by unit commanders who personally trusted them, had undergone training, and had received appropriate equipment. Leadership was also better, with a higher proportion of officers and NCOs per harka than in regular units.[134]

---

[129] Mathias, 1998, pp. 137, and 142–143.

[130] Mathias, 1998, p. 123.

[131] Horne, 1978, p. 255.

[132] Gortzak, 2009, p. 329.

[133] Gortzak, 2009, p. 330.

[134] Gortzak, 2009, pp. 327–328.

As in any counterinsurgency, the French were most successful when their opponents made mistakes. Hence, they did particularly well in regions where the population had been targeted by the FLN.[135] In some instances, the social and economic work undertaken by SAS in remote and poor areas of the country also seems to have contributed to rallying the population to the French side—but the fact that the FLN itself had difficulties reaching these remote areas may have played a role as well.[136] The French also tried to exploit local rivalries within the communities they were trying to reach out to, but these efforts did not always prove successful.[137]

A recurring issue was the mistrust of some French officers for the local defense forces with whom they were working.[138] Harkis were under constant surveillance, for fear that they would take their arms to the ALN. One official note urges SAS officers to keep at all times, in every maghzen, at least one FSE on watch day and night to monitor the FSNA personnel and raise the alert if needed.[139] Harkis were prohibited from using certain weapons and barred from certain tasks, including guarding weapons.[140]

Was this distrust justified? Some desertions, with or without arms, certainly took place, and some FSNA were specifically tasked by the ALN to infiltrate local defense groups to gather intelligence about the French.[141] Two particularly serious cases of desertions with arms in the SAS of Yahiaoui and Colbert in November 1958 produced several conclusions, summarized in an official document as follows: FSE cadres were in insufficient numbers, were not always qualified, and in some cases had been assigned to the SAS against their wishes; some SAS did not follow closely enough the rules on how to recruit and

---

[135]Gortzak, 2009, p. 324.

[136]Gortzak, 2009, p. 325.

[137]Gortzak, 2009, p. 330.

[138]Gortzak, 2009, p. 329.

[139]Minister of Algeria Robert Lacoste, 1958.

[140]Hautreux, 2006, p. 38.

[141]Ageron, 1995, p. 15.

verify the background of FSNA personnel—or were missing the relevant instructions on how to do this properly; some SAS held too many weapons,which were not always stored securely; and SAS were poorly connected to military units, delaying intervention should an attack occur.[142] Other high-profile cases reinforced the general tendency toward suspicion. In March 1960, it was found that some members of the "Commando Georges" were providing the enemy with weapons, ammunition and uniforms.[143] A harka ("Force K") organized by the French under the code name "Blue Bird" (*Oiseau bleu*) eventually turned to the ALN after receiving 300 rifles and submachine guns.[144]

Available figures however show that desertions of local defense forces were rare: 1.57 per thousand in 1956, 0.34 in 1960, 0.45 in 1961.[145] Archival data suggests that they were generally lower than desertion rates for regular forces over the period 1955 to 1961.[146] Figures are not necessarily reliable, however. There may have been some degree of underreporting of desertions for local defense forces.[147] Some "desertions" may also have been simply harkis quitting their job, which was allowed in theory at any time. [148] Additionally, some operational failures may have been unduly assigned to the harkis' responsibility. Horne (1978) mentions an incident where harkis' "treachery" was blamed for an ambush that was mostly due to poor tactics.[149]

Distrust between harkis and their officers worsened in 1961, once it became progressively clear that the French would agree to a peace settlement, potentially leaving their local defense forces unemployed and exposed to FLN reprisals. Harkis increasingly received threats from

---

[142] Guigue, undated.

[143] Ageron, 1995, p. 15.

[144] Horne, 1978, p. 256.

[145] Gortzak, 2009, p. 319.

[146] Faivre, 1995, p. 255.

[147] Faivre, 1995, p. 255.

[148] Hautreux, 2006, p. 38; Gortzak, 2009, p. 318, note 35.

[149] Horne, 1978, p. 255.

members of the surrounding communities.[150] The number of desertions with arms doubled between mid-1960 and mid-1961, resulting in several harkas of suspicious loyalty being disarmed.[151]

Conclusion

Local defense forces were intensively used by the French during the Algerian war, for numerous purposes and under many names. The overall figures are subject to caution, since not all forces were active at a given time and historians' assessments differ. Cassidy (2006) establishes the total contribution of FSNA to the French military and security effort at 150,000 regulars and auxiliaries.[152] Gortzak (2009) gives a figure of "up to 180,000 Muslims . . . at any one time during the conflict."[153] Hautreux (2008) give an estimate of 100,000 at a given time and perhaps 200,000–400,000 during the entire war.[154]

The main benefits of these forces are summarized by Cassidy (2006): an exponential increase in the forces viable to prosecute counterinsurgency; better knowledge of the terrain and environment; and more actionable intelligence about the enemy and enemy sanctuaries.[155] Harkis' value, however, was not limited to better scouting and intelligence. Some proved to have high combat value, especially when a number of factors were present: careful selection, good working conditions (in the form of a pay and package that made little difference between the harki and his FSE equivalent), good command, and proper training. The successful use of harkis in Challe's *commandos de chasse* amply proves that under the appropriate conditions, local defense forces could successfully play an offensive role as well.

---

[150] Ageron, 1995, p. 15.

[151] Ageron, 1994, p. 4.

[152] Cassidy, 2006, p. 53.

[153] Gortzak, 2009, p. 308.

[154] Hautreux, 2008, pp. 49–50.

[155] Cassidy, 2006, p. 59.

CHAPTER FOUR

South Vietnam

Over the course of the counterinsurgency in South Vietnam, numerous efforts were made to create local defense forces, typically via paramilitary formations. The United States provided support to some of these forces, either directly or indirectly. In some cases, the United States provided the initial impetus for the creation of the force. The two most important U.S. efforts to provide local defense forces are the Civilian Irregular Defense Group (CIDG) program and the Combined Action Platoon (CAP) program. While quite similar in intent, the programs were substantially different in both general form and in the role the United States played in supporting them. The third component of building local defense in South Vietnam was the expansion of paramilitary local defense formations before and during the so-called Accelerated Pacification Campaign (APC), launched in the wake of the 1968 Tet Offensive.

Civilian Irregular Defense Groups

The CIDG grew out of a contact between the Central Intelligence Agency (CIA) and "a young volunteer . . . doing economic development work among the Rhade, the principal tribe around the Darlac provincial capital of Ban Me Thuot."[1] This young volunteer, David Nuttle, who

---

[1] Ahern, 2001 (declassified 2006), p. 44. Ahern's research is the official CIA history and draws on numerous interviews with CIA personnel as well as his own experience as a case officer in Vietnam.

was known to the Rhade as "Mr. Dave," spoke the Rhade language and was extremely knowledgeable about their affairs. Nuttle met a CIA case officer from Saigon station's Military Operations Section (MOS) and, in April 1961, he was debriefed by the MOS chief, Gilbert Layton. Layton saw a potential to mobilize the Rhade in their own defense by providing for their needs, which the Government of Vietnam (GVN) had previously neglected. Layton proposed to CIA Chief of Station William Colby a program to arm and train the Rhade to resist the burgeoning insurgency in South Vietnam.[2]

Layton's proposal was accepted and expanded by Colby in May. However, training and arming tribesmen whose relationship to the central government of Vietnam was contentious (at best) was politically sensitive. Colby negotiated an agreement with Ngo Dien Nhu, the security chief for South Vietnam and brother of President Ngo Dien Diem, to move forward by stipulating the participation of Vietnamese Special Forces (VNSF) in the program.

Colby had been cultivating this relationship with Nhu since 1960 when Colby was deputy Chief of Station. Nhu was a difficult partner, given to long disquisitions and obstreperous behavior. However, his agreement was vital to the creation of any local defense force, most especially one involving the troublesome ethnic minorities. Colby's careful cultivation of Nhu, along with his persuasion of U.S. Ambassador Elbridge Durbrow, demonstrate the political skill that the CIA sought to promote in its officers and that is vital for managing local defense forces.[3]

After securing additional permission from Darlac provincial officials, which required yet more negotiation by CIA officers, Layton initiated discussions with the Rhade using "Mr. Dave" and a U.S. Special

---

[2] This account of CIA and Special Forces involvement with the Montagnards is drawn principally from Ahern, 2001, pp. 44–62; Kelly, 1973, pp. 20–33; and 5th Special Forces Group Headquarters, 1970, pp. 83–124. 5th Special Forces Group Headquarters (1970) is a declassified Special Forces internal history that was reprinted in 1996. Note that Kelly appears to have relied on the internal history, so the two sources are not independent. See also Prados, 2003, pp. 83–88; Stanton, 1985; Ives, 2007; and Hickey, 1982, pp. 7–89.

[3] On Colby and Nhu, see Ahern, 2000; and Ahern, 2001, pp. 135–136. Colby's own description of his relationship to Nhu is discussed in Colby, 1989, pp. 31–35 and 89–90.

Forces medic (Sgt. First Class Paul Campbell, aka "Dr. Paul") as his interlocutors. The two surveyed the area, providing medical treatment as they sounded out local leaders. In the fall of 1961, the two men suggested the village of Buon Enao as the site to initiate the program.

This program, named the Civilian Irregular Defense Group (CIDG) program by Colby in late 1961, brought in a small U.S. Army Special Forces team (an "Operational Detachment Alpha" or "ODA" in military parlance) along with VNSF soldiers to train the villagers. Director of Central Intelligence (DCI) Alan Dulles had also signed off on the program at this point, bringing additional funding. The program, which combined economic and medical civic action with the training of village defense forces, quickly took off, drawing in more U.S. and Vietnamese Special Forces over the course of 1962 while remaining firmly under the sponsorship of CIA.[4] Layton and his MOS proved adroit not only at employing CIA resources, which were scarce but required few approvals, but also at exploiting other underutilized resources.[5]

In addition to the disaffected Montagnards of the Central Highlands, the CIA station and U.S. Special Forces engaged the Catholic minority of South Vietnam. Beginning in early 1962, the station armed and trained the followers of militant Catholic priests using CIA resources and U.S. Special Forces ODAs alongside VNSF and, in the case of one ethnic Chinese priest, Nationalist Chinese Special Forces. Known colloquially as "the Fighting Fathers," this program also grew rapidly throughout 1962.[6]

The CIA/Special Forces program sought only to have villagers defend themselves. The Special Forces trained village defenders in basic small arms, and they were expected to fight only if attacked. Otherwise

---

[4] In addition to the CIDG program proper, CIA initiated another program known eventually as "Mountain Scouts" among the Montagnards. It was more of an offensive irregular warfare program than the essentially defensive CIDG. See Ahern, 2001, pp. 64–71; and Kelly, 1973, pp. 33–34.

[5] See Ahern, 2001, pp. 53–54 and 56–58 for examples.

[6] Ahern, 2001, pp. 73–77; Kelly, 1973, p. 33.

they remained at home to live and work. The bulk of these defenders had limited combat capability.[7] Only a small mobile strike force was trained and paid for full-time operations, and even this was intended to patrol the area between villages or quickly support villages under attack, rather than to conduct offensive operations.

"Defensive" was not synonymous with "inactive," as the program relied heavily on local patrolling and intelligence collection. As a U.S. Special Forces history describes it, CIDG defense

> [c]onsisted of small local security patrols, ambushes, village defender patrols, local intelligence nets, and an alert system in which local men, women, and children reported suspicious movement in the area. . . . Strike force troops remained on the alert in the base center at Buon Enao to serve as a reaction force, and the villages maintained a mutually supporting defensive system wherein village defenders rushed to each other's assistance.[8]

The program expanded rapidly after Buon Enao was established. In April, there were 40 villages incorporated into CIDG around Buon Enao with about 1,000 village defenders and a 300-man strike force. By July 1962, the program had 3,600 village defenders and 650 men in strike forces across the Central Highlands. By August over 200 villages were in the program, and by November it had armed 23,000 men (including both village defenders and strike forces). In less than a year, a small army of local defenders had been successfully established with only 24 ODAs and a relative handful of CIA personnel.[9]

At this point, however, the Army bureaucracy intervened. With the establishment of a full Military Assistance Command, Vietnam (MACV) in February 1962, the Army began to move beyond the relatively small-scale efforts of the previous Military Assistance Advisory

---

[7] Ahern, 2001, pp. 53–54.

[8] Kelly, 1973, p. 28.

[9] Ahern, 2001, p. 57; Kelly, 1973, pp. 26–29; 5th Special Forces Group Headquarters, 1970, pp. 85–89. Ahern lists 24 ODAs operational in November 1962, while 5th Special Forces Group Headquarters (1970) lists 26—this difference might reflect that two of the ODAs were at the new base at Nha Trang rather than in the field.

Group (MAAG). Part of this expansion was to establish a special war-fare branch in the operations section of MACV staff. MACV then arranged that both the CIA and MACV would jointly control the CIDG program, which was using Army troops (though funded and supported by the CIA). By June of 1962, a decision was jointly reached in Saigon and Washington that the CIDG program had expanded so much that it was no longer covert and should be fully military (i.e., no CIA involvement).

The transfer of the program from CIA to MACV was known as Operation SWITCHBACK, incorrectly implying that the programs had previously belonged to MACV. Attitudes toward the transfer did not fall neatly along bureaucratic lines. Some in the CIA felt the trans-fer should take place, as Saigon station had limited resources and man-power. DCI John McCone was an early advocate of transferring CIA counterinsurgency programs to the military. Officers at the working level of CIA were split, with some wanting to divest such a relatively overt program while others felt the military would distort the CIDG's mission. However, the ostensible beneficiary of SWITCHBACK, MACV commander General Paul Harkins, felt that the CIA should continue to run the program because it was not ready to transition.[10]

Harkins was particularly concerned about losing the CIA's sen-sitivity to political dynamics in South Vietnam and the station's criti-cal relationships with GVN officials. His concern was echoed by the commander of Special Forces in Vietnam, Colonel George Morton. Morton was also worried about logistics, as he was losing CIA's flexible and effective support and was forced to turn to the expanding bureau-cracy of MACV.[11]

Ultimately, those fearing the failure of the CIDG after SWITCH-BACK were proved correct. MACV proved unable to manage the political dynamics between the provincial and central government and between the lowland Vietnamese and the highland tribes required to make CIDG viable. During SWITCHBACK, the number of villages in the program expanded rapidly even as the quality of the training

---

[10] Ahern, 2001, pp. 97–99.

[11] Ahern, 2001, pp. 102–103.

and support fell.[12] This focus on speed of expansion and total number of villages rather than quality of the village militia was consonant with an approach that emphasized quantitative rather than qualitative measures of success.

Buon Enao, the first and most developed of the CIDG sites, was in disarray by late 1963 since tension between the GVN and the Rhade tribe was not managed.[13] The assumption made by many in the program "was that American assistance and advice was only present to fill a gap—until Vietnamese assets could be built up to assume responsibility." However, this assumption proved deeply problematic. When Buon Enao was turned over to the GVN in September 1962, pay for the strike force was not forthcoming and U.S. organizations had to continue to pay the bills. Rather than local security, the central concern of GVN officials seemed to be disarming the CIDG defenders. This ran counter to everything the defenders had been taught and worsened the relationship between GVN and defenders.[14]

The problems at Buon Enao were not isolated. According to an internal U.S. Army Special Forces study, the transfer of Buon Enao "revealed many of the problems which [had] plagued turnovers right down to 1970."[15] These problems worsened dramatically in 1964, as CIDG units mutinied against the GVN in September and December. The mutineers killed dozens of South Vietnamese involved in the program. Although the situation was eventually defused by CIA and U.S. Special Forces, it indicated the decay of the program.[16]

Equally tellingly, the emphasis on what operations were to be undertaken as part of the program was reversed. The official history of the Special Forces in Vietnam bluntly states: "By the end of 1964 the Montagnard program was no longer an area development project

---

[12] Kelly, 1973, pp. 37–41.

[13] Ahern, 2001, p. 114; Kelly, 1973, pp. 43–44.

[14] 5th Special Forces Group Headquarters, 1970, pp. 128–129; quotation on p. 128.

[15] 5th Special Forces Group Headquarters, 1970, p. 128.

[16] Ahern, 2001, pp. 180–182; 5th Special Forces Group Headquarters, 1970, pp. 63–64. The most detailed account of the September mutiny can be found in the latter document, pp. 100–115.

in the original sense of the term. There was a shift in emphasis from expanding village defense systems to the primary use of area development camps or centers (CIDG camps) as bases for offensive strike force operations."[17]

This shift to offensive operations was accompanied by the gradual conventionalization and standardization of strike force units. This in turn led to a "growing tendency to utilize CIDG units as conventional forces, a task they were neither trained nor equipped to carry out."[18] Combined with the shifting of camps far from their homes, this misuse contributed to "recruiting problems and high AWOL and desertion rates."[19]

Combined Action Platoons

The second major U.S. effort to support local defense in South Vietnam began a few years after the CIDG. This effort, developed by U.S. Marines, sought to enhance the quality of an existing South Vietnamese local defense force rather than creating one from scratch. The Popular Forces (PF) were recruited from villages to provide local security. The Regional Forces (RF) were recruited to provide a provincial-level force that could supplement PFs in areas that were under especially great insurgent pressure. These were paramilitary formations that were formally part of the Army of the Republic of Vietnam (ARVN), although they frequently received little support from other conventional ARVN units or MACV. This absence of effective local security was deeply problematic. Writing of two joint U.S.-ARVN campaign plans (*Hop Tac* and *Chien Thang*) in 1964, a U.S. Army historian noted:

> A critical failing of both Hop Tac and Chien Thang was the continued inability of paramilitary and local police forces to provide local security. Main force Viet Cong and North Vietnam-

---

[17] Kelly, 1973, pp. 33–34.

[18] 5th Special Forces Group Headquarters, 1970, p. 92.

[19] 5th Special Forces Group Headquarters, 1970, p. 236.

ese Army (NVA) units openly challenged the government inside South Vietnam and encountered little trouble in overcoming lightly armed, poorly disciplined, and partially trained South Vietnamese territorials: the Regional and Popular Forces.[20]

The Marines had begun to consider local defense forces even before they were committed to South Vietnam in large numbers. Most notable was Edward Forney, a retired Marine general, who was serving as the Public Safety Advisor in Saigon. Forney had served two years in Haiti during the 1930s and had worked with the Gendarmerie there. In a conversation in February 1963 with Marine Corps chief of staff (and soon to be Commandant) Lieutenant General Wallace Greene, Forney called for an approach similar to earlier Marine experience:

> The Marine Corps should get into the Vietnam job with both feet and that it should be a real grass roots level operation, not tied in with the MAAG; but rather an effort to be linked with the Civil Guard, the Self-Defense Corps, and the local Militia in the village and boondock level. This would be similar to the Guardia effort in Nicaragua or the Gendarmerie operation in Haiti and Santo Domingo.[21]

The limited Marine contingent of 1963 was unable to execute Forney's idea, but the idea would be revisited later, when Marine combat units were introduced in South Vietnam. Two battalions from the 9th Marine Expeditionary Brigade (MEB) landed at Da Nang in March 1965, initially to provide security for the large airbase there. The 9th MEB was commanded by Brigadier General Frederick Karch, the assistant division commander (ADC) for the 3rd Marine Division.[22]

Karch was initially forbidden to conduct offensive operations against the insurgents. His battalions could only defend the airbase and the terrain immediately adjacent to it, so the Marines began immediately attempting to form relations with South Vietnamese

---

[20] Hunt, 1995, p. 27.

[21] Shulimson and Johnson, 1978, p. 134.

[22] Shulimson and Johnson, 1978, pp. 20–27.

security forces. One of the battalions tried to set up a joint checkpoint with the PF unit. However, this effort was unsuccessful because the PF unit showed up at the checkpoint but then wandered off. Though frustrated by this lack of discipline, the Marines continued to try to build ties to the South Vietnamese security forces.[23]

The limited Marine mission would come to end quickly, following a decision by President Johnson in April that "approved a change of mission for all Marine Battalions deployed to Vietnam to permit their more active use under conditions to be established and approved by the Secretary of Defense in consultation with the Secretary of State."[24] In late April, the Marines began conducting joint patrols around Da Nang and Phu Bai (a nearby airfield and intelligence collection post) with ARVN units. Johnson also decided to reinforce the Marines, so that by the end of April, Karch had nearly doubled his force size.[25] More reinforcements came in May, and a higher headquarters, the III Marine Amphibious Force (III MAF) was established.[26]

The expanding Marine presence and loosened operating guidelines enabled Marine battalion commanders to initiate counterinsurgency operations with an emphasis on local defense.[27] The first major operation was initiated by Lieutenant Colonel David Clement, commanding the 2nd Battalion, 3rd Marine Regiment (2/3). 2/3 held an area overlooking the village of Le My, a cluster of hamlets eight miles northwest of Da Nang. Conversations with the Vietnamese district chief revealed that this village had been swept by ARVN several times but security was never maintained.

Clement resolved to provide security for the village. In early May, he accompanied the district officer on a visit the village, accompanied by 2/3's S-2 (intelligence officer) and the S-2's scouts. This led to a skirmish with the Viet Cong in which one of the scouts was killed. Clem-

[23] Shulimson and Johnson, 1978, pp. 19–20.

[24] National Security Action Memorandum, 1965.

[25] Shulimson and Johnson, 1978, pp. 25–27.

[26] Shulimson and Johnson, 1978, pp. 29–36.

[27] The following account of Le My is drawn from Shulimson and Johnson, 1978, pp. 37–39.

ent realized the village would have to be cleared and a week later, one of 2/3's companies returned and occupied the village. The company then enlisted the villagers in clearing traps and destroying insurgent bunkers. After three days, the PFs, supported by RFs, a province-level paramilitary force, occupied the village proper while the Marines moved to provide security around the village.

In addition, Clement's battalion began working to improve the village. His Marines trained the local PFs, built village defenses, and initiated civic action programs such as medical stations and a school building. The goal of this activity, in the words of 2/3's S-2 (who doubled as civil affairs officer), Captain Lionel Silva, was "to create an administration, supported by the people, and capable of leading, treating, feeding, and protecting themselves by the time the battalion was moved to another area of operations."[28]

Senior Marine officers enthusiastically supported 2/3's approach to counterinsurgency. III MAF commander Major General William Collins remarked that the "Le My operation may well be the pattern for the employment of Marine Corps forces in this area." On a visit to III MAF in mid-May, the commander of Fleet Marine Forces Pacific (FMFP), Lieutenant General Victor Krulak, described the operation at Le My as ". . . a beginning, but a good beginning. The people are beginning to get the idea that U.S. generated security is a long term affair."[29]

Major General Collins was replaced as III MAF commander by Major General Lewis Walt in June. Walt also embraced the pacification mission, famously noting about Da Nang "that over 150,000 civilians were living within 81mm mortar range of the airfield, and consequently, the 'Marines were into the pacification business.'"[30] Walt, though a veteran of high-intensity conflict in World War II and Korea, had been mentored by the generation of Marines who trained local defense forces in the so-called "Banana Wars," recalling "that as a

---

[28] Quoted in Shulimson and Johnson, 1978, p. 38.

[29] Both quoted in Shulimson and Johnson, 1978, p. 39.

[30] Shulimson and Johnson, 1978, p. 46.

young officer he learned the fundamentals of his profession 'from men who had fought Sandino in Nicaragua or Charlemagne in Haiti.'"[31]

Some of Walt's battalion commanders also embraced this Marine approach to developing local defense forces. In addition to Clement, Lieutenant Colonel William "Woody" Taylor, commanding the 3rd Battalion, 4th Marine Regiment (3/4) at Phu Bai, also emphasized the importance of the population.[32] In June 1965, Taylor, acting on advice from his adjutant/civil affairs officer, negotiated with the local ARVN division commander for authority to work with the PFs to secure villages in Zone A, an area north and east of Phu Bai.

Taylor received permission and limited operational control of the PFs in July. His executive officer drew up plans to incorporate a Marine squad into four of the six PF platoons in Zone A. Taylor then briefed the plans to his superiors, including Major General Walt, who gave him permission to proceed and detailed a Vietnamese-speaking Marine 1st lieutenant named Paul Ek from headquarters to assist him in establishing a "joint action company."

The Marines who participated in the joint action company (which Commandant Greene would recognize as an echo of retired Marine General Edward Forney's 1963 suggestion) were all volunteers. Each was personally vetted by 1st Lieutenant Ek, who would command the joint company. He also spent several weeks instructing the Marines about Vietnamese life.

The company was joint but American-dominated. In practice, the Marine squad leader became the combined platoon commander, with the PF commander his deputy. Ek also had a South Vietnamese warrant officer as his deputy. However, the Vietnamese district chief retained administrative responsibility for the unit, while each platoon had to work with the chief of the village it was securing. The Marine platoon commander was therefore called upon "to maintain harmonious relations among his subordinates, the village chief, and his PFs."[33]

---

[31] Shulimson and Johnson, 1978, p. 133.

[32] The following account of the early combined action program is drawn from Shulimson and Johnson, 1978, pp. 133–139.

[33] Shulimson and Johnson, 1978, p. 135.

The unit, renamed the "combined action company" in October, engendered loyalty in both PFs and Marines, with several Marines volunteering to extend their tours.

Other Marine units also began to work with Vietnamese local forces, including the PFs and the RFs. General Walt was a supporter of all these efforts, considering the PFs in particular to be critical to security despite their poor training and equipment. He noted of the PF soldier:

> He had a signal advantage over all others; he was defending his own home, family, and neighbors. The Popular Force soldier knew every person in his community by face and name; he knew each paddy, field, trail, bush, or bamboo clump, each family shelter, tunnel, and buried rice urn. He knew in most cases the local Viet Cong guerrilla band, and it was not uncommon for him to be related to one or more of them by blood or other family ties.[34]

Walt also persuaded the ARVN corps commander to release more PFs to Marine operational control in November, and then persuaded the general to expand the combined action approach to all three Marine areas in January 1966.[35]

The Marine Corps continued to expand the combined action program in 1966, focusing on the platoon element of the program, the CAP, which embedded a Marine squad in a PF platoon.[36] Walt set a goal of 74 CAPs for the end of 1966. However, the desired rate of expansion was not reached. The central limiting factor was not Marine willingness. Rather, PF recruitment and the unwillingness of many Vietnamese province and district chiefs to participate in the program

---

[34] Shulimson and Johnson, 1978, p. 138.

[35] Shulimson and Johnson, 1978, p. 138.

[36] On CAP, see West, 2003; Hemingway, 1994; Peterson, 1989; and Brewington, 1996.

explained the limited expansion of CAPs.[37] The program reached 75 CAP units in mid-1967, Walt's earlier goal for the end of 1966, only six months late in spite of the difficulties the program encountered.[38]

Notably, CAP units rarely if ever relied on firepower other than that of their organic small arms unless they were in danger of being overrun by a massed enemy.[39] Indeed, in 1970 an after-action report from the Americal Division, the Army division that would eventually work with Marine units in the southern part of the Marine area of operations, noted that "Few artillery fire missions were requested by CAPs because team members were inexperienced and lacked confidence in the capabilities of artillery to support them."[40] More likely, the Marines simply felt that artillery support would do more harm than good.

CAP Marines were generally volunteers from line Marine units. The first director of the overall combined action program, Lieutenant Colonel William Corson, described what he sought in CAP Marines:

> The men I wanted to come into the Combined Action Program had to have line experience. They had to know what it meant to take another human being's life, and how to shoot, move, and communicate. That is not to say I was looking for the kill crazy types or psychotics. Sadly, you occasionally run into people like that. On the other hand, I wasn't looking for bleeding heart liberals, either. . . . I also realized that it was not possible to transform these Marines into linguists or cultural anthropologists overnight.[41]

The rigor of selection varied from unit to unit and over time, but the key was a desire in volunteers to help the Vietnamese people. One CAP veteran recalled the recruiting pitch: "Instead of just killing the

---

[37] Hennessy, 1997, pp. 94 and 131.

[38] Hennessy, 1997, p. 111.

[39] See West, 2003, pp. 42–43.

[40] "Operational Report—Lessons Learned," 1970, p. 8.

[41] Hemingway, 1994, p. 50.

enemy . . . you'll have a chance to work with the local people and help take care of them. You'll be a real part of their lives."[42] Training was limited, often just a few weeks of basic Vietnamese culture and specific skills for living in an austere and dangerous environment.[43] Corson noted that he tried to teach CAP Marines "how to eat a meal in a Vietnamese home, how to play elephant chess, how to be accepted in a Vietnamese environment and perform a very difficult mission."[44]

In the wake of the 1968 Tet Offensive, the Marines began working to restore order to the countryside.[45] However, the threat of conventional North Vietnamese Army units limited the expansion of the CAP program. The target for the end of 1967 had been 114 platoons, but only 79 were functional.[46] However, after Tet the Marines resumed expansion (albeit slow) of the program. By July 1968, there were 93 platoons in the program.[47] By the end of the year there were 102 platoons.[48]

The Marines continued to maintain the CAP program as the war continued, although the program's expansion remained slow due to continuing shortages of personnel, both Marine and PF—more the latter than the former. The program reached 114 platoons in August 1969, remaining at that level through March 1970. The number of platoons in the program peaked at about 120 before beginning to decline in July 1970 as the Marines began to withdraw.[49]

CAP units faced a variety of problems that were never fully resolved. One was the danger of infiltration of PF units by insurgents. Not only was this a direct threat, it could also weaken trust between

---

[42] Goodson, 1997, p. 10.

[43] Goodson, 1997, pp. 16–19.

[44] Hemingway, 1997, p. 50.

[45] Shulimson et al., 1997, pp. 607–608.

[46] Shulimson et al., 1997, p. 619.

[47] Shulimson et al., 1997, p. 623.

[48] Shulimson et al., 1997, p. 625.

[49] *Operations of U.S. Marine Forces, Vietnam,* September 1969, pp. 23–24; III Marine Amphibious Force, 1970, p. 2.

the PFs and the Marines.[50] Theft of Marine items, while less danger-ous, also hurt the development of trust and rapport between Marines and PFs.[51]

While some PF members were skilled fighters, the general rule was that even with Marine training the PFs had limited skill and discipline. As one CAP Marine noted, "Sometimes . . . it is difficult to get the PFs to open fire on the VC [Viet Cong]. So we use the PFs as our eyes and ears. It is the Marines who do the actual fighting. You cannot always depend on the PFs to advance with Marines."[52]

Another challenge was that, while as noted earlier, CAP Marines were ideally volunteers, this was not always the case. CAP Marine vet-eran Tom Harvey noted:

A few of the Marines had come from line units and were "gook haters." They should never have set foot in a CAP but in the early days when CAP was "voluntary" the line units sometimes got rid of their [expletive deleted] by sending them to CAP when vol-unteers were requested. . . . While in [CAP] school there was a discussion going on one evening in the large tent where we slept. These were NCOs, corporals and sergeants talking about blowing away civilians. I was sad to hear that most of them favored it. I can only recall one who spoke out in opposition.[53]

Based on extensive interviews and his own experience with CAP, Michael Peterson notes that bad behavior among CAP units, while limited, was real including torture, rape, extortion, and—in at least one case—murder.[54]

For all these challenges, when CAPs functioned effectively they were highly capable. In this respect a more micro-level examination of the CAP program in a single province (Quang Ngai) and a single

---

[50] Goodson, 1997, pp. 88–90.

[51] Peterson, 1989, pp. 93–94

[52] West, 2003, p. 62.

[53] Tom Harvey, email response to interview questions, May 2011.

[54] Peterson, 1989, pp. 89–91.

village in that province (Binh Nghia) is instructive. CAPs were introduced to Quang Ngai province in the summer of 1966. One of the first was at the village of Binh Nghia, with Marines entering the village on June 10.[55] Other CAP units were created in the province throughout the remainder of 1966.

CAPs came to the province relatively late (nearly a year after the first CAP units were formed) for three reasons. First, the Chu Lai base, from which CAP Marines for the province would be drawn, became operational somewhat later than the other bases. Second, permission to expand the program to the area around Chu Lai was given by the ARVN corps commander in January 1966, but he was then fired in March (for unrelated reasons). His firing provoked an intense political crisis in the region—with large protests in the cities and a fear of troop mutiny—that lasted until June. The controversy required mediation by the III MAF commander and essentially halted CAP expansion from March to May since no decisions could be made.[56] Finally, Quang Ngai had a large insurgent presence (though no main force NVA units), making it difficult to find PF units willing to participate. Nonetheless, there were fourteen CAPs in the vicinity of Chu Lai by the end of September 1966 (unfortunately these are not broken out by province in available historical records, but at least one was in Quang Ngai).[57]

Binh Nghia, a village in a northern district of Quang Ngai, was in the Marine area of operations around Chu Lai. A CAP unit was introduced into the village in July 1966. This unit would remain in place for more than a year. For the first year, the CAP unit fought a series of small unit actions with the local insurgents. Under the tutelage of the Marines, the PF unit grew more competent and confident.[58]

---

[55] West, 2003, p. 14.

[56] For discussion of this crisis, see *Operations of U.S. Marine Forces, Vietnam*, May 1966, pp. 27–30. The crisis was most intense and long-lasting in Hue; see *Operations of U.S. Marine Forces, Vietnam*, June 1966, pp. 32–33.

[57] *Operations of U.S. Marine Forces, Vietnam*, September 1966, p. 25. By 1970 there were sixteen CAP units in Quang Ngai. See Peterson, 1989, Appendix A.

[58] West, 2003, passim.

By August 1967, the area around the village was so secure that the insurgents essentially ceased contesting it. In October 1967, after more than two months without seeing an insurgent, the Marines in the CAP unit were relocated to work with another PF platoon.[59] While the insurgency was not eliminated in the area, it had certainly been weakened greatly. Moreover, this had been accomplished by the Marines and locals through small unit actions with minimal firepower, sparing civilians the devastation that firepower often entails.

For Binh Nghia, the Tet Offensive of 1968 proved to be the beginning of the end for insurgent presence. The insurgent unit based in its vicinity was badly mauled during an assault on the provincial capital. While the insurgent unit reconstituted itself, with the exception of a single major attack in the spring of 1968, it was never again a significant force around Binh Nghia. By 1970, the area was so secure that it was designated a "rest and recuperation area," and the PF platoon was relocated to another nearby village.[60]

For all its success, the CAP units at the village of Binh Nghia did have problems. One in particular was the role of local politics. As Bing West notes of those Marines and their PF partners:

> The PFs were organizational orphans. Although they were fighting for their village and their homes, their political ties stopped at the village gate. While they hated the Viet Cong, they also strongly disliked both factions of the VNQDD [the political party dominant in Quang Ngai province]. Their only source of political leverage lay in the presence of their American allies, since they could not rely upon the government of South Vietnam to treat them fairly. . . .[61]

Thus the CAP Marines not only had to fight the insurgency but also had to manage the relationship between the PF platoon and the provincial government.

---

[59] West, 2003, pp. 319–321.

[60] West, 2003, pp. 332–334 and 343–347.

[61] West, 2003, p. 210.

RF/PFs, PSDF, and the Accelerated Pacification Campaign

While CAPs focused on building the capacity of specific PF units in the Marine area of operations, there were also broader efforts by the United States to improve and expand RFs and PFs throughout South Vietnam. Local defense forces were a critical part of the broader pacification campaign directed primarily by MACV Deputy for Civil Operations and Revolutionary Development Support (CORDS) Robert Komer. Beginning in 1967, Komer directed an intensive effort to enhance RFs and PFs. Komer himself claimed

> [i]n a real sense, we were the first ones in the long history of the Vietnam War—though there were several previous attempts—to actually put the territorial security concept of clear and hold and territorial forces on the map on a scale commensurate with the need.[62]

A major component of Komer's effort was to acquire more and higher quality advisers for RF/PFs (referred to somewhat dismissively as "Ruff-Puffs"). In May 1967, there was a ratio of about one U.S. advisor per 1,000 of these local defense forces. In contrast, there was about one U.S. advisor per 23 soldiers in the South Vietnamese Army. The quality of RF/PF advisory personnel was equally lacking due to the preference of many U.S. Army personnel for command or staff rather than advisory assignments.[63]

By the beginning of 1968, Komer had made substantial progress on both fronts. He had secured an increase of over 125 percent in the number of advisors assigned to RF/PFs. In addition, he had successfully lobbied for an incentive package for those willing to accept advisory duty. These incentives included pay and allowance increases as well as crucial credit for command duty, a major factor in an officer's promotion

---

[62] Komer, 1970, p. 63. Emphasis in original.

[63] Hunt, 1995, pp. 106–107.

chances. However, ceilings on U.S. force levels and the decision by the Johnson administration not to call up the reserves continued to limit both the quality and quantity of RF/PF advisors.[64]

In order to expand the reach of the limited number of advisors available, MACV and CORDS created Mobile Advisory Teams (MATs), five-man units that would travel around to provide on-site training to PF and RF units. This training consisted primarily of tactical and weapons training, along with instruction on constructing field fortification and calling for indirect fire support. MATs themselves received special training from a school established expressly to help them deal with "the special problems that faced army officers working with South Vietnamese military forces." Initially at the provincial level, CORDS eventually established a MAT in every district and at every RF/PF headquarters, for a total of 354 teams. In addition, MACV established Mobile Advisory Logistics Teams that worked to improve the RF/PF logistics support.[65]

Assessments of MATs were mixed. Komer and some of his staff at CORDS felt that MATs were incredibly powerful force multipliers, greatly enhancing the capability of tens of thousands of RF/PFs with fewer than 2,000 U.S. personnel. In contrast, Komer thought that while CAP was a good idea in general it was too manpower-intensive, given the limited number of U.S. forces available.[66] Conversely, Andrew Krepinevich argues that these teams, which typically stayed with a given RF/PF unit for roughly a month, were insufficient to truly improve their capability. Instead MATs "reflected the Army's quick-fix approach to counterinsurgency and its desire for quick results."[67]

In addition to working to improve the advisory support to RF/PFs, CORDS and MACV also sought to improve their equipment. In 1967, RF/PFs were frequently at a firepower disadvantage against the insurgents since the insurgency increasingly had AK-47s, light

---

[64] Hunt, 1995, pp. 107–109.

[65] Hunt, 1995, pp. 108–109, quotation on p. 109.

[66] Komer, 1970, pp. 102–103.

[67] Krepinevich, 1986, p. 177.

machine guns, and mortars, while RF/PFs lacked even modern assault rifles. Throughout 1968 and 1969, MACV provided thousands of M-16s, M-60 light machine guns, and M-79 grenade launchers to the nearly 400,000 RF/PFs. An early 1969 assessment argued that roughly 80 percent of RF/PF units had firepower equal to or greater than the insurgents they faced.[68]

In conjunction with the effort to improve RF/PFs, CORDS personnel spearheaded two other initiatives to improve local defense that emerged after the 1968 Tet Offensive. Although the Tet Offensive had a variety of effects, two effects of relevance to local defense were that it both galvanized the previously lethargic and divided South Vietnamese government to take action and it greatly reduced the insurgency's military capability. The former enabled the creation of a new local defense force and the latter enabled the rapid expansion of security.

The new local defense force was called the People's Self Defense Force (PSDF) and it was enabled by a mobilization decree from the South Vietnamese government that required service in it from essentially all military-aged males not already working in a security force.[69] PSDF was part time and the members were not well armed. At best, PSDF units were equipped with admittedly "hand me down" weapons, such as M-1 carbines released from RF/PF units as those units received M-16s. At worst, they received no weapons at all.[70] Nonetheless, the PSDF expanded rapidly, reaching 1.4 million by June 1969.[71]

The expansion of local security was accomplished under the Accelerated Pacification Campaign, an intensive effort from mid-1968 to early 1969 intended to expand government presence and security into the countryside. While the offensive set back efforts to build local security, it also created an opportunity. Tet, as noted earlier, forced many insurgent units to go on the offensive in ways that exposed them en masse to the full weight of U.S. and South Vietnamese firepower.

---

[68] Hunt, 1995, pp. 154 and 214.

[69] Komer, 1970, p. 82; Hunt, 1995, p. 152.

[70] Hunt, 1995, pp. 154 and 199.

[71] Hunt, 1995, p. 253.

This resulted in at least a temporary vacuum in the insurgent presence that could be exploited.

The APC, among other things, sought to coordinate security forces in order to protect the expansion of government presence. In areas deemed "relatively secure," the new PSDF, working with PF platoons, would provide security within villages and hamlets while the RF would conduct mobile operations around these hamlets. In areas deemed "contested or enemy-controlled" the PF alone would provide security within the hamlets and villages while the South Vietnamese Army and RF would conduct mobile operations around them.[72]

As with MATs, assessments of the effectiveness of the APC were mixed. During this period 227 RF companies and 710 PF platoons were stationed in these contested or enemy-controlled areas, which many in MACV believed indicated the growing capability of the South Vietnamese to take and secure territory at the local level. However, given the short duration of the campaign it was unclear if these local security forces could maintain the gains of the APC.[73]

Local security after 1969 continued to face serious challenges. The insurgency, realizing the threat posed by these local security forces, began to target RF/PFs and PSDF heavily in 1969 and afterwards. Indeed, based on casualty rates, service with the RF/PF was more dangerous than service in the South Vietnamese or U.S. military.[74] By 1971, as U.S. withdrawal was well under way, over half of local defense forces were still rated as unsatisfactory. Desertion from RF/PFs, despite an improvement since 1967, still remained a serious problem. Even in areas known for relatively high quality RF/PFs, corruption, poor leadership, and "padding of payrolls" were cause for complaint.[75] Ultimately the ability of local defense in South Vietnam after U.S. withdrawal was rendered moot when the invasion by conventional North Vietnamese formations in 1975 made RF/PFs and PSDF irrelevant.

---

[72] Hunt, 1995, p. 158.

[73] Hunt, 1995, pp. 203–204.

[74] Hunt, 1995, pp. 218 and 253.

[75] Hunt 1995, pp. 258–259.

Conclusion and Assessment

The various programs of the United States in Vietnam clearly show both the pros and cons of local defense. While the CIDG suffered from a focus on quantity rather than quality of recruits, the CAP benefited, after a difficult start, from a commitment of the Marines to be closely involved in the program and to provide a degree of leadership that had been missing previously. This change of strategy paid off, with insurgents lastingly deserting some areas patrolled by the Marines and the CAPs. Both programs, however, shared some challenges that the United States could not successfully overcome. Recruiting, in particular, proved difficult, especially when local defense forces were required to operate far from their home bases.

The American experience in Vietnam shows that various organizations present different strengths and weaknesses in setting up and training local defense forces. In the case of the CIDG, the CIA's flexibility and intimate knowledge of Vietnamese political dynamics were critical assets that were lost during the SWITCHBACK transition. Meanwhile, the Marines proved to be the best choice to motivate and provide discipline to the PF and RF.

The difficulties that the CIDG encountered when it transitioned to the GVN illustrate the classic dilemma that governments experience when dealing with local defense forces. While they certainly need the help of these local forces to counter insurgencies successfully, they also fear that such forces may develop into a counter-power capable of successfully competing with the country's central authority. This concern is particularly acute when local defense forces are built around ethnic minorities that may have a vested interest in correcting the political balance of power in their favor—hence, the disastrous transition of the CIDG to a government of Vietnam intent on disarming rather than integrating them. The fact that PF and RF were already formally part of the ARVN seems to have facilitated their transition. Both programs suggest that future integration of local defense forces into the regular state apparatus needs to be addressed early on by both the intervening country and the central government.

CHAPTER FIVE

Oman

In the late 1960s, the British government faced a dilemma in the Middle East. It was committed to a policy of retrenchment from its former protectorates and colonial possessions "east of Suez." At the same time, it retained real interests in the region due to both Cold War security concerns and the booming development of energy resources there. This dilemma essentially meant that British foreign and security policy in this arena would be one of "limited liability," with minimal but non-zero resources committed to ensuring the survival of friendly regimes.[1]

The strengths and weaknesses of this approach would become apparent in Oman in the 1970s as a Communist insurgency developed in the southern region of Oman known as Dhofar. Oman had been a client state of the British since the 19th century, and in the late 1950s Britain had supported the sultan against a separatist movement in northern Oman. However, the challenge in Dhofar was substantial: British support was constrained even as the insurgency received external support from the Communist bloc and had sanctuary in neighboring South Yemen.

The British military was of necessity closely partnered with the Omanis. In particular, it relied heavily on local tribal defense forces (*firqat*), many of whom had formerly been insurgents.[2] The firqat, along with improvements in the regular Omani military, the Sultan's

---

[1] See Dockrill, 2002, and Ladwig, 2008, for an overview.

[2] *Firqat* (singular *firqah*) in Arabic means simply "groups" or "units." For clarity throughout, *firqat* will be used for both singular and plural references.

well as limitations in arms and equipment, meant that despite posing a real threat to the government's control of Dhofar, the DLF was nonetheless restricted in the size and scope of its operations.[10]

In late 1967, however, South Yemen, led by Communist affiliates, gained independence and quickly became a sanctuary and source of support for the DLF. South Yemen, eventually called the People's Democratic Republic of Yemen (PDRY), particularly empowered the Communists within the DLF, which was renamed the Popular Front for the Liberation of the Occupied Arabian Gulf (PFLOAG). Although this did not end divisions within the insurgency, the new front was reinvigorated by the sanctuary and supply (the latter frequently flowing from China) from the PDRY. In 1968 it began campaigns in the Jabal that eventually pushed the SAF and the government out of the area. The SAF was clearly on the defensive throughout 1968–1969, and popular support for PFLOAG was growing. By April 1970, the government of Oman faced a "truly wretched" situation in Dhofar, according to the new Chief of the SAF, Brigadier John Graham.[11]

The Coup and Emergence of Local Defense, 1970–1971

Sultan Sa'id bin Taymur, determined to keep Oman, particularly Dhofar, in the 19th century, was seen by many as the primary cause of the insurgency. It is thus not surprising that there was discussion of removing him from power, but nothing came of it until 1970. The most likely candidate to replace him, his son Qaboos, was kept under virtual house arrest.[12]

Qaboos was British-educated and had served in the British army, so not only were his views of government more progressive than his father's but he also had a better understanding of modern military requirements and strong ties to the British army. With at least tacit

---

[10] Peterson, 2007, pp. 194–197; and Ladwig, 2008, pp. 66–67.

[11] Peterson, 2007, pp. 194–197 and 212–227; Hughes, 2009, pp. 280–281. The Graham quotation appears on p. 227 of Peterson, 2007.

[12] Jeapes, 2005, pp. 27–29.

support from the British government, Qaboos began building links to individuals in Oman's capital of Muscat, as well as Salalah in Dhofar, sometime in the spring of 1970. On July 23, 1970, Qaboos launched a coup against his father that was very nearly bloodless. His father went into a comfortable exile in London, where he died in 1972.[13]

Sultan Qaboos moved quickly both to consolidate his own authority and to reverse his father's problematic policies. He released political prisoners, promised greater openness and development, and began traveling the country to meet the people. In November, he announced that henceforth Dhofar would no longer be the sultan's personal property but would become a regular province of Oman. He also declared an amnesty for those willing to lay down their arms and began to further modernize the SAF, including incorporation of the previously independent Dhofar Force.[14]

To assist in the training and modernization of the SAF, Qaboos accepted an offer by the British to dispatch members of the elite Special Air Service (SAS) to Oman. The SAS had previously aided Oman in combating the 1950s insurgency in northern Oman but Sultan Sa'id had rejected SAS assistance in Dhofar. SAS participation was initially to be training only and therefore operated under the cover designation British Army Training Team (BATT). By early 1971, 70–80 SAS troopers were in Oman under the command of Major Tony Jeapes. Jeapes had previously participated in the British campaigns in Malaya and northern Oman, so he was familiar with both counterinsurgency and Oman.[15]

Sultan Qaboos' reforms, in conjunction with an information service set up with BATT assistance to publicize those reforms, rapidly began to have an effect. In September 1970, three dozen insurgents surrendered to the government, accepting amnesty. More would follow over the coming months as Dhofari nationalists realized that the sultan had essentially alleviated all their grievances. Indeed, the prime insti-

---

[13] Peterson, 2007, pp. 238–241; Allen, 1987.

[14] Peterson, 2007, pp. 242–245; Ladwig, 2008, pp. 72–73.

[15] Peterson, 2007, pp. 245–247; Jeapes, 2005, pp. 17–19. For more on Jeapes' previous experience, see Hosmer and Crane, 1963, p. xx and passim.

gator of the initial rebellion surrendered in December 1970, arguing that Sultan Qaboos "was willing to give them even more than they demanded."[16]

These surrenders caused the fractures in PFLOAG to open wider and provoked the Communists within the insurgency to take oppressive steps to prevent further defection. Combined with the atheism and anti-tribalism of the Communists, these oppressive measures began to erode popular support for the insurgency. Within a short period, the insurgency had been transformed from one about broadly held Dhofari grievances toward the old sultan to one seeking to change Dhofar in ways too radical for most Dhofaris.[17]

In addition to changing the nature of PLFOAG, these former insurgents, whom BATT termed Surrendered Enemy Personnel (SEPs), provided a golden opportunity, if treated well. They had intimate knowledge of local terrain and social relationships that the BATT and the regular SAF could never hope to match, combined with an understanding of the insurgency's inner working. If they could be convinced to join the government, units composed of SEPs could be a powerful security force, particularly if combined with the military skill and discipline of the BATT's SAS troopers.[18]

The opportunity to form such a unit came soon after Jeapes' arrival in Oman. He was approached by Salim Mubarak, a senior insurgent commander who had surrendered in September 1970. Mubarak offered to form a firqat of former insurgents to fight against PFLOAG if Jeapes and BATT would provide training and equipment. The firqat would be drawn from across tribes, a highly progressive step in Omani society, and would be called the Firqat Salah ad Din (FSD) after the great Muslim general.[19]

This first firqat was trans-tribal, with the intention being to break down tribal rivalries. This was, not coincidentally, the way PFLOAG

---

16 Peterson, 2007, p. 245.

17 Peterson, 2007, pp. 251–253; Jeapes, 2005, pp. 38–39.

18 Hughes, 2009, pp. 283–284.

19 Peterson, 2007, pp. 247–249; Jeapes, 2005, pp. 38–41.

organized itself. The members of this first firqat had been insurgents, so it was believed they would be amenable to such an organization, which proved at first to be the case. The FSD was formed with an initial manning of 32; its base was at the coastal town of Mirbat. Partnered with seven SAS troopers from BATT and armed with FN FAL rifles, the FSD began to train for operations. During this period, FSD members located clandestine PFLOAG members in Mirbat and the nearby town of Taqa.[20]

In February 1971, the FSD undertook its first action against the small village of Sudh about 20 miles east of Mirbat. A mixed force of FSD and BATT troops seized the town without incident and the FSD began to ingratiate themselves with the population, teaching the children to sing pro-FSD songs and conversing with the adults. Within days the town had been won over to the side of the new sultan and the government of Oman.[21]

The FSD also began to exchange letters with the PFLOAG force in the area around Sudh, led by a man known as Qartoob. After Qartoob declared he would not join the government, the FSD, taking advantage of a remark by the messenger about Qartoob's location and their intimate local knowledge, sent a party out that located and surrounded him. The FSD offered him a choice of negotiation or death; he wisely chose the former. After a few days of discussion with members of the FSD and BATT, his entire insurgent group of 140 had agreed to rally to the new sultan and roughly a quarter of them, including Qartoob, joined the FSD. Almost without firing a shot, the FSD in a few days had not only retaken Sudh but had also eliminated a major insurgent group and expanded its own size substantially, all due to the FSD's local knowledge.[22]

The firqat concept began to expand in this period as well. Two significant Dhofari tribes, the Bayt Kathir and Mahra, volunteered to form their own firqat. However, they stipulated these new firqat would only have members from their particular tribes. BATT and the govern-

---

[20] Peterson, 2007, p. 257; Jeapes, 2005, pp. 60–67.

[21] Jeapes, 2005, pp. 71–76.

[22] Peterson, 2007, p. 257; Jeapes, 2005, pp. 76–81.

ment of Oman accepted these terms and two new firqat were formed with each operating in its particular tribal area. They were soon joined by another based around the village of Taqa.[23]

However, the original firqat, FSD, after a successful operation to start re-establishing a government presence on the Jabal, began to experience friction. Qartoob did not share the trans-tribal outlook of the original FSD leadership and in April 1971 he and his tribesmen refused to serve in the FSD any longer. After discussion they left the FSD, which was reduced to its original size. This marked the end of trans-tribal firqat, and all subsequent firqat were organized along tribal lines.[24]

Despite this friction, firqat operations continued to produce results. In May 1971, a member of the FSD led the unit to a major insurgent supply dump following a substantial engagement with enemy forces. As one historian of Oman notes of this operation: "The FSD not only served as the eyes and ears of the operation, but also carried the brunt of the fighting, with more than one member showing exceptional bravery." However, other firqat performance was less impressive, in large part due to lack of training.[25]

In addition to their role as ground forces, firqat members were also useful as so-called "flying fingers." Although many Dhofaris, including firqat members, were illiterate and unfamiliar with maps, they had detailed knowledge of their local environment. In order to take advantage of this knowledge without using maps, BATT and SAF hit upon the solution of taking firqat members up in a helicopter where they could pinpoint locations. These locations were then passed to pilots for airstrikes. The accuracy of the subsequent strikes was frequently very good and, because the firqat members could point out insurgent

---

[23] Peterson, 2007, pp. 258–259; Jeapes, 2005, pp. 57–70.

[24] Peterson, 2007, p. 259; Jeapes, 2005, pp. 111–113.

[25] Peterson, 2007, pp. 259–260; quotation on p. 260.

meeting spots, often devastating. Indeed, Jeapes would later claim that intelligence indicated that PFLOAG ". . . feared the Flying Finger more than anything else the SAF could do at the time."[26]

The effectiveness of the flying fingers also highlights the close cooperation between the SAF and the firqat. While there was a certain degree of rivalry and friction, in part because most SAF personnel were not from Dhofar, the two generally worked well together. This was no doubt due in part to the fact that SAF was staffed principally with British officers, who had a common understanding and bond with their BATT counterparts. By mid-1971, the model that SAF and BATT developed called for "concurrent 'clear and hold' or pacification activities . . . using firqat to pacify and then protect populated areas, backed up by a combination of a 'hearts and minds' campaign and psyops efforts."[27] This campaign was conducted by BATT units called Civil Action Teams in conjunction with the government of Oman, which would eventually create a Dhofar Development Committee to coordinate this work.

The firqat continued to expand, increasing the demand for BATT personnel to train, advise, and support them, so the sultan requested a second SAS squadron. This second squadron was approved and dispatched by the British government in the fall. This brought the total SAS personnel in Oman to over 100, representing half of the 22 SAS Regiment (though this force level would not be continuously sustained).[28]

In the meantime, the firqat continued to have internal problems resulting from friction with BATT and each other. In an attempt to resolve these disputes, Sultan Qaboos held an audience with all the firqat leaders and selected other members. They aired their grievances,

---

[26] Jeapes, 2005, pp. 68–69; quotation on p. 69.

[27] Peterson, 2007, p. 267.

[28] Peterson, 2007, pp. 267–268.

which he then dismissed, telling them to listen to the advice of BATT personnel. He did give formal commendations to those he deemed to be performing well while sidelining or firing problematic commanders.[29]

Once BATT personnel were in place and some of the firqat issues had been settled, the SAF and BATT decided to launch a major effort to reestablish government presence on the Jabal. Known as Operation JAGUAR, it brought together both SAS squadrons, and five firqat totaling about 300 personnel, and three regular SAF companies, along with artillery and some tribal quasi-police known as askaris. After fierce fighting and arduous marching, the force managed to establish a permanent base, known as White City to BATT and as Madinat al-Haq to the Omanis. White City "became the centre of the first permanent government social service on the Jabal, with a clinic, school and shop opened by the Sultan."[30]

In November, firqat members at White City issued an ultimatum, as they wanted to take cattle and goats from there to the coastal city of Salalah for sale. If this demand were denied, they would refuse to fight. While some in the SAF considered this a mutiny, BATT and the Omani government officials took a longer view, realizing they would win loyalty by acceding. The Sultan gave another lecture about discipline to the firqat leaders, but then a cattle drive from White City was authorized. Wryly and appropriately named Operation Taurus, this brought valuable cattle to market, winning "hearts and minds" while stimulating the economy. Indeed, over the next few years the price of cattle boomed as economic development took place and demand exceeded supply.[31]

---

[29] Peterson, 2007, pp. 269–270.

[30] Peterson, 2007, pp. 275–277; quotation on p. 276. See also Jeapes, 2005, pp. 135–141.

[31] Peterson, 2007, p. 277; Jeapes, 2005, pp. 142–143 and 173. Jeapes (2005) notes that the cost of a cow increased more than twelvefold between 1971 and 1977. Peterson claims another cattle drive in February 1972 was called Operation Taurus; it is not clear if both were called Taurus or if one of the authors is mistaken.

The Tide Turns and Local Defense Matures, 1972–1974

As 1972 began, the momentum PFLOAG had gained after its Communist allies came to power in South Yemen had been reversed. However, there was still much to be done to secure Dhofar, particularly in the Jabal where White City remained the sole permanent base. The firqat would continue to develop and play a major role in the counterinsurgency campaign over the next two years.

Over the course of 1972, additional firqat were established, bringing the total to eleven. They varied in size from platoon to company with a total strength of about 700. A higher headquarters for the firqat (Headquarters Firqat Forces) was established to ensure coordination and supply.[32]

This higher headquarters was also intended to handle the transition of firqat from close partnership with BATT while they were being established to one that drew support from SAF. In 1974, the SAS squadron commander in Oman described "the three phases in a firqat's development":

> The first phase is raising and training them, sorting out their tribal problems and establishing a leader. The second phase is the main operational phase, getting a company or battalion of SAF, and as many BATT as we can, and establishing them in their tribal area and helping them clear it. The third phase is getting the civil action going, a well drilled, a clinic, school and shop built, and so on. That's when we withdraw and hand over to Firqat Forces, freeing our men to start again with another firqat.[33]

Following this hand-off, each firqat was intended to have a liaison officer to Firqat Forces to provide oversight. Getting appropriate personnel could be difficult, however, so many of these officers were contracted former SAS troopers.[34]

---

[32] Peterson, 2007, p. 295.

[33] Jeapes, 2005, pp. 166–167.

[34] Jeapes, 2005, p. 166.

rades in the east."[47] Only the west still had a significant insurgent presence, so the campaign plan for 1975 called for pulling most of the SAF and allied units from the east and center to clear the west. This would leave security in the east and center in the hands of the firqat.[48]

The ability to gather intelligence through local knowledge of terrain and population remained the premiere ability of the firqat. Tony Jeapes, who was promoted to command the 22 SAS Regiment and returned to Oman in 1974–1976, noted the frustration of one SAF battalion commander who, due to prejudice against irregulars, refused to work with the firqat. As a result, his battalion could not get intelligence and was totally unable to make contact with the insurgents. SAF commanders lacking this prejudice had substantially less trouble with intelligence.[49]

At the same time, there were already questions about the role and future of the firqat. Jeapes describes the changed nature of the firqat from 1970 to 1975:

> They're more mature, they understand more about the realities of life, what is feasible and what isn't, and their leaders tend to be older men than before. The firqat leaders are becoming little warlords, in fact. They control everything that goes on in their own areas, the grazing, watering, the sale of government food, everything. As soon as they're established in their areas you can see them change from being soldiers to politicians. Most of them spend far less time on the jebel than they should because they are all down here in Salalah, where the political decisions are made.[50]

The campaign plan for 1975 was executed so effectively that by October insurgents in the west had been all but totally cut off from their support and sanctuary in the PDRY. In contrast to the fierce resistance in January, an October offensive against the Shirshitti caves

---

[47] Peterson, 2007, p. 359.

[48] Peterson, 2007, p. 362.

[49] Jeapes, 2005, pp. 232–233.

[50] Jeapes, 2005, p. 167.

ended quickly with only a single casualty (caused by a landmine). More than 100 tons of munitions were captured there, and within weeks the PLFOAG high command ordered a major withdrawal of forces out of the west as surrenders swelled.[51]

With the insurgent presence effectively eliminated in the west by the end of 1975, in 1976 BATT and the firqat, along with SAF, focused on eliminating the remaining rebels in the center and east. Surrenders continued, including major insurgent commanders. In the east, fewer than 60 insurgents remained with no heavy weapons, forced to operate in groups of four or five.[52] At Oman's National Day celebrations in 1976, the sultan announced the war was over.[53]

Although this declaration was a bit premature, the end was in sight, raising questions about the future of the firqat. A 1974 assessment by a British official had argued the firqat should be reconstituted as a formal National Guard once the bulk of the fighting was over. Members would then be given four choices: retiring with a pension, transferring to SAF, vocational training for a new occupation, or serving in the new National Guard. Another concern was that the firqat leaders would undermine the traditional authority structure given the clout they had amassed during the war. This was to be addressed by strengthening the government's administrative capacity. A final concern was limiting tribal feuds, which might thrive in the firqat.[54]

From 1976 to 1979, the war slowly wound down. Contacts with insurgents became more and more infrequent and always on a small scale. At the end of 1978, the SAF decided that of the 13 bases it had been maintaining on the Jabal (up from zero in 1971) it would retain six, transfer six to the firqat and close one. In 1979 there were only four contacts with insurgents and the war functionally came to an end.[55]

---

[51] Peterson, 2007, pp. 375–376.

[52] Peterson, 2007, pp. 380–382.

[53] Allen, 1987, p. 63.

[54] Peterson, 2007, pp. 392–393.

[55] Peterson, 2007, pp. 395–397.

the local community would often raise funds for a unit to purchase supplies and the like. In contrast, the poor-quality units had minimal community support, and some would simply disintegrate over time.[8]

Positive Assessments of Civil Defense

Some in the Salvadoran military felt that Civil Defense had been a major contributor to security. The former commander of the Salvadoran Army's 2nd Brigade felt that it was a major obstacle to the insurgency despite some problem units that damaged the reputation of the program. He relayed an anecdote about a Civil Defense unit spontaneously created by a Mr. Beltran after his illegitimate son tried to get him to join the insurgency. Mr. Beltran fought off an assassination attempt with a single-shot shotgun before going to the army for help. The army provided some training and nineteen rifles for the 300 men of Mr. Beltran's unit. This unit began to accompany units from the 2nd Brigade on operations, helping provide manpower and intelligence. This unit, well motivated if not well armed, was a valuable asset according to this officer.[9] The former commander of the Salvadoran army's 1st Brigade likewise believed that the program had been a major success, particularly since the Civil Defense was motivated by a genuine desire to resist the insurgency rather than by a salary.[10]

Similarly, many from MILGRP felt Civil Defense was also crucially important. Col. John Waghelstein, MILGRP commander in 1982–1983, noted that it was imperative to "have a well trained or

---

[8] Defense Intelligence Agency (DIA), 1987, pp. 17–19. The commander of the U.S. Military Group in El Salvador in 1987, Colonel John Ellerson, noted 104 "new" Civil Defense sites and 220 "old and new" sites in September 1987. The "old" sites presumably included Territorial Service sites not assessed by DIA. See Manwaring and Prisk, 1988, p. 337.

[9] Interview with Colonel Oscar Casanova Vejar, in BDM International, 1988, Vol. 5, pp. 1–6.

[10] Interview with Colonel Leopaldo Antonio Hernandez in BDM International, 1988, Vol. 5, p. 7.

adequately trained civil defense to provide the first line of defense."[11] He also felt that Civil Defense was a good metric for progress in the war. If Civil Defense recruiting, training, and combat performance were all improving along with the rate at which army units were coming to the aid of Civil Defense, then the war was probably going well.[12]

Colonel Ellerson likewise believed Civil Defense was a "cheap combat multiplier," particularly after the army had broken up large guerrilla units.[13] He remarked that small guerrilla units of three to eight men could be handled by "our little guys without very many teeth."[14] Ellerson also described how insurgent written propaganda and the insurgent radio station, Radio Venceremos, described the Civil Defense units as "a major irritant."[15]

Probems with Civil Defense

One of the main concerns that emerged with Civil Defense in El Salvador was its potential as a cover for right-wing "death squad" activity. While the exact extent to which Civil Defense was a cover for such activity is unknown, even the appearance that the program was associated with such action was detrimental. Not only did it provide a propaganda boon to the insurgency, but it also amplified the concerns of many Salvadorans that Civil Defense was just a new name for the same old repressive practices. U.S. military advisers, who had adopted a "train the trainer" approach to Civil Defense, were unable to provide the close oversight necessary to convincingly ensure that these units were not used in this fashion.[16]

---

[11] Interview with Colonel John Waghelstein in BDM International, 1988, Vol. 6, p. 81. See also Waghelstein, 1994.

[12] Interview with Waghelstein, 1988, p. 7.

[13] Interview with Colonel John Ellerson in BDM International, 1988, Vol. 6, p. 81.

[14] Interview with Ellerson, 1988, p. 86.

[15] Interview with Ellerson, 1988, p. 88.

[16] Walker, 1990. See also Schwarz, 1991, p. 54.

and recruited some members from previous despised militias only contributed to making Civil Defense more suspicious in the eyes of the population.

While there are mixed assessments of the Municipales en Accion program, it shows that there may be utility to focusing on small-scale development projects directed by locals. It also shows the role that organizations other than the U.S. military and intelligence agencies—here, USAID—can play in developing an approach that addresses not only the needs of those who participate in local defense forces but also the communities around them.

Civil Defense, however, was equally distrusted by the government and the regular army of El Salvador. As a result, it did not receive the support it needed and was not given the means to be an effective ally of the state in counterinsurgency. Its intelligence value, too, was undermined by this lack of trust, as the government did not even bother to exploit what little information was collected on the ground by Civil Defense units. Poorly monitored, lightly trained, and considered with suspicion by those it was meant to support—state and nonstate actors alike—Civil Defense proved of limited use in the response to the Salvadoran insurgency.

CHAPTER SEVEN

Southern Lebanon

From 1978 to 2000, Israel sought to counter the influence of the Palestinian Liberation Organization (PLO) and, after 1983, Hezbollah, by arming, training, and financing local defense forces in southern Lebanon. These local forces included the Free Lebanon Army (FLA), the FLA's successor, the South Lebanon Army (SLA), and the Home Guards.[1] The Israel Defense Forces (IDF) generally augmented these forces with commando raids, air strikes, and indirect fire from 1978 to 1982, and local defense forces were used as auxiliaries to occupying IDF units from 1982 to 2000. The zones controlled by these local defense forces originally provided Israel with a useful buffer between its northern border and southern Lebanon. The SLA also conducted patrols, manned checkpoints, and participated in joint and unilateral operations. Yet, the SLA ultimately crumbled due to internal deficiencies and external pressure.

Israel's use of armed proxies in southern Lebanon provides useful lessons with respect to local defense programs writ large. Without strong accountability mechanisms, Israeli-backed forces in the South were able to carry out brutal and abusive operations. Additionally, the force was not representative of the operating environment's local milieu; the disproportionate number of Christians in the SLA rendered it incongruent with the Shi'i majority in the South. Overwhelming

---

[1] This chapter focuses on Israeli efforts to establish local defense forces in southern Lebanon. It does not cover Israel's support for Phalangist militias or its broader support for elements of the Maronite political establishment in Beirut. For an exploration of Israel's historical ties to Lebanese confessional minorities, see Eisenberg, 2010, pp. 10–24.

reliance on economic incentives in recruiting the force also hampered the extent to which its members could be expected to resist adversary influence. Israel also failed—or outright refused—to navigate the complex relationship between the SLA, the Lebanese government, and its occupying forces. Simply put, Israeli efforts in the South did not necessarily seek to extend the writ of the central Lebanese government in Beirut.[2] The local forces were thus viewed by many elements of the Lebanese government as renegades at best, traitors at worst.

This chapter begins by providing a rudimentary timeline of Israel's major military operations in South Lebanon from 1978 to 2000. Next, it analyzes Israel's funding, training, and coordination with local defense forces in South Lebanon by focusing on two separate periods: the 1978–1982 period, during which these forces acted on behalf of IDF units generally residing outside of Lebanon, and the 1982–2000 period, when they augmented and eventually partnered with their Israeli counterparts. It concludes by exploring what lessons should be gleaned from Israel's experience with local defense.

Israeli Operations and the Evolution of the Security Zone

Israel's local defense efforts occurred in the context of numerous other military instruments. Indeed, Israel's strategy to evict terrorist threats from Lebanese territory has historically consisted of a number of components: commando raids, air strikes, and direct occupation. To provide context for our analysis of Israel's experience with local defense forces, this section briefly outlines major Israeli operations in southern Lebanon from 1978 to 2000.

Southern Lebanon has long been home to an array of anti-Israel militant groups. From approximately 1971 to 1982, the Palestinian Liberation Organization (PLO) utilized areas in the South to train its cadres, conduct cross-border attacks on northern Israel, and plan

---

[2] This became particularly apparent in the wake of Bashir Gemayel's assassination in September 1982, which caused Israel's objective of installing a "pro Israeli government" in Beirut to "founder." See Norton, 2000, p. 23.

spectacular attacks on international targets. Hezbollah (1983–present) similarly used—and has continued to use—areas in southern Lebanon to stage attacks on Israeli military and civilian targets.

Coupled with continued rocket attacks on Israel's northern settlements, a Fatah-led terrorist attack on Israeli soil that left 38 dead spurred Israel to launch its first major operation in southern Lebanon. The operation, which was launched in March 1978, was originally known as Operation Stone of Wisdom but was eventually dubbed Operation Litani.[3] Between 7,000 and 10,000 Israel Defense Force (IDF) soldiers mobilized to push PLO forces north of the Litani River. After successfully doing so, Israeli forces withdrew, and 5,250 United Nations Interim Force in Lebanon (UNIFIL) peacekeepers were deployed to the country.[4] As it gradually withdrew from Lebanese territory, the IDF employed a Greek Catholic, Major Saad Haddad, who was in charge of what was then known as the Free Lebanese Army. The FLA was to act as a "hold" force for the 10-kilometer-deep "security zone" that constituted a buffer between PLO forces and the Israeli border.[5]

Operation Litani failed to sustain its initial successes. Anticipating a limited ground incursion, PLO forces retreated north of the Litani River ahead of time.[6] After the Israeli drawdown, approximately 800 PLO militants were able to reclaim their bases in the area despite the presence of the security zone.[7]

Simmering tensions and continued aggression between the PLO and the IDF, coupled with an assassination attempt on an Israeli ambassador in London, led Israel to launch Operation Peace for Galilee in 1982.[8] Able to capitalize on territory held by the FLA, the 75,000–78,000-strong IDF quickly swept through southern Lebanon

---

[3] Yaniv, 1987, p. 71.

[4] Coban, 1984, p. 96.

[5] Sela, 2007, p. 59.

[6] Yaniv, 1987, p. 72.

[7] Bavly and Salpeter, 1984, p. 57.

[8] For an in-depth exploration of why Israel invaded in 1982, see Kaufman, 2010, pp. 25–38.

and laid siege to Beirut.[9] The PLO, defeated militarily and devoid of Lebanese popular support because of its high-handed treatment of the population, eventually relocated to Tunisia.[10] As the last of PLO forces fell back in 1985, the IDF established a slightly expanded security zone that at its deepest point was 15 km wide. From 1985 to 2000, Israel maintained a presence of 1,000–3,000 troops, partnered with an SLA force that grew to approximately 2,500–3,000 fighters.

The IDF's success conducting conventional military operations targeting a foreign militant group based in Lebanon did not translate into success against the local guerrilla adversary it was now facing as it occupied the South. Although elements of the Muslim population in southern Lebanon originally welcomed the Israeli invaders due to their weariness of PLO misconduct, this sentiment was short-lived in the face of a foreign military occupation.[11] Growing disenfranchisement and frustration with Israeli heavy-handedness and Christian favoritism (which sprang from Christian resistance to the primarily Muslim PLO) helped generate a fierce brand of Shi'i militancy in southern Lebanon. Employing a range of innovative tactics, the Shiite militias Amal and later Hezbollah effectively targeted IDF and SLA forces alike.[12]

Israel also launched two major operations during the 1990s, both of which aimed to disrupt Hezbollah activities and pressure the southern population and the Lebanese government to rein in the militant group. In July 1993, Israel launched Operation Accountability, a week-long series of bombardments that were partially aimed at convincing "influential powers" in Lebanon to "curb Hezbollah's activities."[13] Facing growing international pressure and continued rocket attacks,

---

[9] Gabriel, 1984, p. 80.

[10] For more on the PLO's decision to flee from Beirut, see Khalidi,1986; and Sayigh, 1997, pp. 522–543.

[11] Ehud Barak, the former Prime Minister of Israel, noted, "When we entered Lebanon . . . there was no Hezbollah. We were accepted with perfumed rice and flowers by Shia in the south. It was our presence there that created Hezbollah" (Norton, 2007, p. 33).

[12] For more on Hezbollah's military activities, see Norton, 2007; Jaber, 1997; Blanford, 2011; O'Shea, 1998, pp. 307–319; and Cambanis, 2010.

[13] Helmer, 2007, p. 56.

Israel reached a verbal ceasefire agreement with Hezbollah, wherein both sides agreed not to attack civilian targets.[14]

As the ceasefire began to break down, Israel launched Operation Grapes of Wrath in 1996, a 17-day-long operation that also included the heavy bombardment of southern Lebanon.[15] In the wake of this operation, a series of written agreements between Israel, Lebanon, Hezbollah, and Syria stipulated that Hezbollah "will not carry out attacks . . . into Israel" and Israel "will not fire any kind of weapon at civilians or civilian targets in Lebanon."[16] But a combination of Hezbollah resilience and efficacy, not to mention growing Israeli public opposition to the occupation of Lebanon, led then–Prime Minister Ehud Barak to order the unilateral withdrawal of IDF troops from southern Lebanon in May 2000.

The Consolidation of the Free Lebanon Army, 1978–1982

From 1978 to 1982, Israel began providing gradually more overt and regular military and civilian assistance to primarily Maronite communities in southern Lebanon. Initially, these efforts were fragmentary, and the local forces were undisciplined and abusive. Eventually, Israel was able to consolidate and expand local defense efforts under Saad Haddad's FLA, which served as the de facto security force for the small buffer zone along the Israeli border. Yet, as the force's mandate grew and recruitment problems persisted, it adopted overly expedient recruitment practices to expand the size of the force at the expense of community rapport and military capability.

Israeli military contact with Lebanese Christian communities in the South has its roots in first Arab-Israeli War, after which a number of Maronite Christians approached Israeli officers and asked to join

---

[14] Helmer, 2007, p. 56.

[15] This included the infamous Israeli shelling of a United Nations compound in Qana, killing 106 and injuring 118 civilians.

[16] Sobelman, 2010, pp. 56–57.

the IDF.[17] In 1958, the IDF supplied weapons and ammunition to citizens in southern Lebanon, due to fears of a Syrian invasion.[18] During Lebanon's 1976 civil war, a number of Christian villages in southern Lebanon also requested humanitarian and military support from Israel.[19] With the disintegration of the Lebanese Armed Forces (LAF) along confessional lines during the mid to late 1970s, Israel also found recruits for a local defense force among the large number of demobilized Christian soldiers who had returned to their home villages.[20]

Israel thus began offering military and humanitarian assistance to Christian communities in southern Lebanon in a more systematic fashion. For one, Israel armed a number of demobilized Christian soldiers commanded by the IDF through communications with small outposts in south Lebanon.[21] These units were offered military training in small camps on the Israeli side of the border.[22] A number of Maronite Christian villages were offered access to medical, transportation, and communication services in Israel. This was the beginning of what became known as the "Good Fence" policy.[23]

The initial force's military activities reflected its piecemeal and undisciplined nature. Operations originally focused on securing the Christian majority enclaves in the South.[24] Eventually, these forces lashed out at Shiite villages as well, sometimes with indiscrim-

---

[17] Instead of being allowed to join the IDF, some of these Maronites were trained in "mine-setting operations" and "other forms of harassment" by Israeli forces. Many later joined the Lebanese Armed Forces (Hamizrachi, 1988, pp. 14–15).

[18] Hamizrachi, 1988, p. 19.

[19] Sela, 2007, p. 59; Hamizrachi, 1988, pp. 45–75.

[20] Beydoun, 1992, p. 40.

[21] Beydoun, 1992, p. 42.

[22] Hamizrachi, 1988, p. 66.

[23] Phares, 1996, pp. 21–30.

[24] For a detailed account of these operations, see Hamizrachi, 1988, pp. 63–75; and Phares, 1996, pp. 21–30.

inate force.[25] On top of this, military leaders in the three enclaves were prone to internal squabbling, which compromised their ability to coordinate military activities.[26]

To consolidate these efforts, Israel turned to Major Saad Haddad,[27] a Greek Catholic, and Major Sami Shidiak, both members of the LAF. The latter's unwillingness to take part in military operations and the local population's rejection of his authority rendered him far less reliable in the eyes of the IDF.[28] Having first made contact with his Israeli paymasters in 1976, Haddad thus assumed the brunt of the responsibility for the three enclaves.[29] During his tenure, Haddad was not known for his bravery, often made tactical errors, lacked control over his men, and was unable to make any decisions without Israeli support and instruction.[30] Sadly, Haddad appears to have been the best of a bad lot.

Israeli military training and provision of aid to Haddad's forces did help to bolster Israel's intelligence collection activities in the short term, however. Mossad, the Israeli intelligence agency, had previously established contacts with Lebanese Christians in the South and built relationships with military officers "in order to receive intelligence information."[31] Many of the fighters in the Kleia village, for example, had long-standing covert ties to Israeli intelligence.[32] In addition, Haddad's men were eventually able to establish ties with Muslims who provided valuable intelligence on PLO deployments.[33] Lebanese civilians

---

[25] Phares, 1996, pp. 21–30.

[26] Hamizrachi, 1988, pp. 80–81.

[27] It should be noted that Haddad was not the only Lebanese army official to have ties with Israel. See Hamizrachi, 1988, pp. 63–64.

[28] Hamizrachi, 1988, pp. 107–108.

[29] Hamizrachi, 1988, p. 80.

[30] Hamizrachi, 1988, p. 138.

[31] Hamizrachi, 1988, p. 64.

[32] Hamizrachi, 1988, p. 70.

[33] See, for example, Hamizrachi, 1988, p. 122.

who provided information when crossing the "Good Fence" further augmented intelligence collection.[34]

Haddad's initial actions focused on clearing lines of communication between the three Christian enclaves that were separated by PLO-held areas.[35] Abusive behavior again ensued to varied degrees. In Hanin, Haddad's forces used Israeli cover to clear out the village, inflicting considerable damage.[36] In cleared areas, Haddad established "committees" that were responsible for organizing the defense of their villages, the commanders of which were given weapons and communications equipment and were incorporated into Haddad's force.[37] Yet, once villages had been cleared of PLO militants, looting was commonplace.[38] That said, Haddad did attempt to facilitate civilian assistance for Lebanese villages through requests to Israeli military leaders.[39] During Operation Litani, Haddad's men held territory cleared by the IDF but were similarly accused of acting with excessive force, particularly against civilians.[40]

Seeking to better organize and consolidate their efforts, in May 1978 Israeli defense officials decided to implement a "local defense system" in the outh that "assured the villagers that the safety of their village lay in the hands of their own men."[41] This included embedding Israeli military and civilian advisors in southern Lebanon to support and advise local defense forces.[42] With Israeli support for his men intensifying, Haddad subsequently renounced his ties to the Lebanese government and declared his territory the "Free State of Lebanon" in

---

[34] Hamizrachi, 1988, p. 66.

[35] Beydoun, 1992, p. 43.

[36] Beydoun, 1992, p. 43.

[37] Hamizrachi, 1988, pp. 86–87.

[38] Hamizrachi, 1988, pp. 86 and 90.

[39] Hamizrachi, 1988, p. 81. Though this aid favored Christians, some of it also went to Muslims.

[40] Beydoun, 1992; see also Hamizrachi, 1988, pp. 167–168.

[41] Hamizrachi, 1988, p. 180.

[42] Kaufman, 2010, p. 31.

April 1979. Consequentially the Lebanese government disowned and eventually court-martialed Haddad.[43] Rather than being tasked with merely defending Christian enclaves in the South from PLO influence, the FLA now had a much broader mandate that included securing the 8–12-km-deep border strip.[44] This required FLA units to be more mobile and confessionally diverse to cover territory that would inevitably include non-Christian villages. As such, a recruitment drive was instituted through the village committees, which were given recruit quotas proportional to the population of each village.[45]

Recruitment difficulties impeded the force's expansion. For one, previous abuse by Christian militias in the South likely continued to resonate locally, while the FLA also had a reputation for extortion, excessive drinking, and abuse.[46] Coercive recruitment practices also led many males to flee their home villages for fear of being forced to join.[47] Another hindrance appears to be tied to fears of what would happen to males once they joined. Indeed, those suspected of having previously been "pro-Palestinian" were excessively beaten as part of their "re-education."[48]

Rather than treating the underlying causes of recruitment shortages and other grievances related to the force, Israel focused almost exclusively on providing economic incentives to potential recruits. During this period, Israel instituted a new system through which, in addition to the roughly $150 monthly salary an FLA soldier received, a family member of each soldier could cross the border to work in Israel to earn around $300 a month. For villages hit hardest by the economic hardships of the 1970s, these incentives were likely adequate to encourage a significant growth in force numbers, at least temporarily.

---

[43] Jabir, 1999, p. 387.

[44] Sela, 2007, p. 60.

[45] Beydoun, 1992, p. 45.

[46] Jabir, 1999, p. 375.

[47] Beydoun, 1992, p. 44.

[48] Beydoun, 1992, p. 45.

Despite efforts to expand the size and confessional inclusiveness of theFLA, problems still persisted regarding the FLA's confessional makeup. Israel mandated that FLA's officers for Muslim units be non-Muslims.[49] Thus, Shiites tasked to patrol their home villages were under the command of Christian officers, as were most of the checkpoints within the security zone.[50] Beyond prestige, the post of village commander offered significant financial benefits, as commanders could draw fees by issuing licenses and permits.[51]

The FLA's expansion, eventually yielding around 2,500 men, also attracted individuals whose local ties and dedication to ridding southern Lebanon of PLO influence were tenuous.[52] Indeed, Haddad's force consisted of demobilized soldiers, unemployed males, foreign fighters,[53] Christian militants (some of whom were from outside the area),[54] and even children.[55] As a result, motivations for joining the FLA varied significantly. Although many were indeed motivated by the considerable financial incentives provided by Israel, other more parochial concerns also played a role. For one, inter-clan rivalries encouraged some to join the FLA. As noted in the firsthand account of Ahmed Beydoun, "if a clan was induced to allow one or more of its members to join the SLA [successor to the FLA], rival clans would feel threatened . . . it was enough for a few members of one clan to join the SLA for other clans to encourage a few elements of their own to join as well."[56] In other cases, issues related to sectarian worries and prestige between villages also helped convince young men to join.[57]

---

[49] Jabir, 1999, p. 375.

[50] Jabir, 1999, p. 387.

[51] Hamizrachi, 1988, p. 170.

[52] On the total SLA personnel, see Byman, 2011, p. 219.

[53] Indeed, Haddad apparently acknowledged that he had fighters from Britain, Holland, and America fighting alongside his men. See Jabir, 1999, pp. 387–388.

[54] Jabir, 1999, p. 388.

[55] Hunter, 2006; see also Jabir, 1999, p. 388.

[56] Beydoun, 1992, p. 45.

[57] Beydoun, 1992, p. 45.

Despite renewed Israeli efforts to professionalize through improved training of the force, the FLA still appeared undisciplined and predatory. In many cases, FLA soldiers imposed taxes on the local population, extracting fees for everything from inheritance to successfully locating kidnap victims.[58] In other cases, the force showed a lack of restraint. For example, Haddad's forces shelled a UN position when its "tax and intelligence collecting activities were . . . being undermined."[59] Ultimately, however, the most problematic dimension of the force was the fact that the FLA existed as a parallel security force that would compete with, rather than be incorporated in, the LAF. This helped doom the FLA to eternal dependence on the Israelis and left it with no firm institutional footing.[60]

Thus, the 1978–1982 period witnessed the IDF gradually consolidating and organizing its local defense efforts in the South. Although these forces were initially responsible for small enclaves, their mandate expanded in the wake of Operation Litani. This need for an expanded and more diverse local force contributed to overly expedient recruitment practices and overreliance on economic incentives. Because of this, not all of the FLA forces were motivated by the desire to quell militancy in the South or stabilize their home villages. The recruitment of FLA members was sometimes harsh. Formerly pro-Palestinian Lebanese were allowed in after "reeducation, which consisted mainly of beatings."[61] Conversely, Christian members of the SLA sometimes "did not behave in seemly fashion with the young ladies of the villages."[62] This combination of abuse and bad behavior made recruitment difficult and created resentment against the FLA.

That said, from 1978 to 1982, the security zone was pacified and generally cleared of militants, while some locals from the zone provided

---

[58] Jabir, 1999, p. 386.

[59] Norton and Schwedler, 1993, p. 71.

[60] Byman, 2011, pp. 219–220.

[61] Beydoun, 1992, p. 45.

[62] Beydoun, 1992, p. 46.

areas.[76] On top of this, the Shi'i clergy issued numerous fatwas condemning any collusion with the IDF, which included participating in the Home Guards program.[77]

The combination of the Home Guards' disintegration and the death of Saad Haddad in 1984 led Israeli military leaders to restructure their approach to local defense in southern Lebanon.[78] Abandoning the Home Guards entirely in the aftermath of Saad Haddad's death, Israeli forces placed Antoine Lahad, a retired Lebanese army brigadier general, in charge of the FLA. The force was subsequently renamed the South Lebanon Army.[79] By this time, defections had brought force numbers down to roughly 800, and eye witness accounts described them as being "unqualified" and lacking discipline.[80] In 1985 the force was around 60–65 percent Christian; but by 1986, 95 percent of the Shiites had fled from the force and very few Sunnis and Druze remained, making the SLA overwhelmingly Christian.[81] Thus, Lahad inherited, and initially struggled with, an extremely flawed local security force.

To address the SLA's considerable deficiencies, from 1986 to 1988 Israel implemented a number of new measures that aimed to enhance the force's capabilities and local ties. Training was expanded from four to twelve weeks, with leadership courses given to commanders, and first aid, communications, and demolition courses given to rank-and-file fighters.[82] The force was also restructured in the form of a more hierarchical, regular military force and given improved weaponry and equipment to track down and neutralize explosives.[83]

---

[76] "Muhawalatayn li-Ightiyal Mas'ulin fi 'al-Haras' Qadhifa," 1984.

[77] Yaniv, 1987, pp. 241–242.

[78] Yaniv, 1987, pp. 241–242.

[79] It is highly likely that a number of the rank-and-file Home Guards were incorporated into the SLA.

[80] Jabir, 1999, pp. 391–392.

[81] Jabir, 1999, pp. 395–396.

[82] Jabir, 1999, p. 396.

[83] Yaniv, 1987, p. 243; "Middle East, South Lebanon Army—A Profile," 2000.

Despite the longer, more intense training regimen and eventual recruitment of new of Shi'i fighters, SLA forces still were notorious for being abusive and undisciplined. This may have been due to the difficulties in recruiting, which in turn meant many of the recruits were of low quality. Some of the Christians had also been radicalized against Muslims.[84] SLA gunners were injudicious in their use of fire-power on Muslim villages, leading the IDF to replace them with IDF crews in the western sector, and eventually assume control of all artillery fire.[85] Arbitrary arrests, incommunicado detention, torture, and indiscriminate use of deadly force were some of the many other grievances expressed against the SLA during the 1990s.[86] The SLA also still forcibly recruited child soldiers[87] and a number of the older SLA fighters were outright unfit for duty.[88]

The IDF and SLA also tried again to make the force more representative of the confessional make up of southern Lebanon. In order to foster stronger connections between Lahad's soldiers and Muslim residents, a recruitment drive focused on gaining Muslim support and preventing the force from becoming overtly Christian was implemented.[89] Lahad himself argued in May 1984 that his force was "for all sects in the South, for the Christians as well as the Muslims."[90]

Yet, recruitment practices were again flawed. Israel used what was locally called a policy of "terror and temptation," wherein it would threaten to close border gates[91] or take "revenge" if locals did not

---

[84] Beydoun, 1992, pp. 45–46.

[85] Blanche, 1997.

[86] This was perhaps most notorious in the SLA's infamous al-Khiam prison. See Human Rights Watch, 1999; and Lavie, 1997, pp. 34–36.

[87] Hunter, 2006.

[88] One observer noted, for example, "Most checkpoints are manned by senior citizens, seriously out of shape, or kids aged 15 or 16." See ". . . and Its Crumbling Militia," 1998.

[89] Jabir, 1999, p. 400.

[90] "Lahad Tafaqqad Mawaq' wa Zara al-Salahiya, 1984.

[91] Jabir, 1999, p. 400.

cooperate and join the force.[92] Economic incentives were also a component of Israel's recruitment strategy during this period. In the 1990s the salary of SLA fighters rose considerably: By the end of 1997, a fighter's salary was as high as $600, compared to LAF soldiers' $360.[93] These efforts yielded a force whose motivations again varied from economic to other parochial concerns.[94]

At the same time Israel increased its civilian assistance to communities in the South. For example, Israel offered $250,000 for a school in southern Lebanon and carried out other building projects and medical assistance programs.[95] Additionally, roughly 2,500–5,000 Lebanese workers (all of whom had to be sponsored by an SLA fighter) earned between $350–$750 a month by working in Israel.[96] But much of this assistance was confined to Christian villages, and attempts to reach beyond these confessional divides were "offset" by the IDF's operations in Muslim villages, which often left them in ruins.[97]

These practices did manage, however, to reconstitute the SLA's dwindling force numbers despite the SLA's poor reputation. Indeed, the bleak economic atmosphere of southern Lebanon pushed many Shiites to "take the Israeli shilling" and join the SLA.[98] In a few weeks in April 1984, the SLA's numbers rose by roughly 300 fighters.[99] By 1987, the SLA had 2,700 fighters, and in 1988 one of the commanders was a Shiite.[100] During the 1990s, the SLA force had a Shi'i majority,

---

[92] Hirst, 1999, p. 15; Hunter, "2006; "Tahqiq li-Reuters min al-Mantaqa al-Hadudiya," 1985.

[93] Jabir, 1999, p. 407.

[94] Jabir, 1999, p. 400.

[95] Jones, 1997, p. 96.

[96] Barak and Sheffer, 2006. p. 254.

[97] Jones, 1997, p. 96.

[98] Jones, 1997, p. 93.

[99] "Nisbat Tatawwu' fi 'al-Jaysh al-Janubi' Ila Irtifa,'" 1984.

[100] Jabir, 1999, p. 410.

though it still likely fell short of the roughly 80 percent Muslim population in the South.[101]

Israel also tried to more systematically capitalize on the intelligence-gathering capabilities of their local force during this period. Near the end of 1982, Israeli Shin Bet operatives were deployed to South Lebanon to begin establishing more robust HUMINT collection activities.[102] The IDF's Aman was also responsible for disseminating this and other intelligence to its fielded units.[103] Both Shin Bet and Aman established intelligence apparatuses within the SLA.[104] The IDF's Mabat (a Hebrew acronym for "security apparatus") consisted of easily identifiable units within the SLA tasked with gathering field intelligence.[105] For its part, Shin Bet established Shabbak Section 501 in 1995, units tasked with establishing HUMINT sources in the South.[106] SLA soldiers employed in Shabbak Section 501 were paid more than $1,000 per month—a large raise from the SLA's typical $300–$600 monthly salary.[107]

These attempts to institutionalize intelligence collection through the SLA yielded poor results. For one thing, SLA intelligence collection methods remained abusive. Stories of beatings and torture were commonplace, as were seemingly random arrests.[108] Further, the information the IDF received through SLA channels was not reliable. A Shin Bet operator reflected, for example, "We never knew whether to believe the SLA people. They were caught in a thicket of dual loyalties and feared what would happen to them in the event of an Israeli withdrawal, so it was impossible to make them a party to vital information.

---

[101] Venter, 1996.

[102] Black and Morris, 1991, p. 395.

[103] Jones, 2001, p. 10.

[104] Jones, 2001, p. 9.

[105] Bergman, 1999a.

[106] Jones, 2001, p. 10.

[107] Jones, 2001, p. 10.

[108] Black and Morris, 1991, p. 397.

ple, a first-hand account noted the "self-service" SLA checkpoints, wherein motorists would physically move the blockades before passing through, while an SLA fighter hunkered down in a bunker and "waved warily."[125] A small uprising, described as a "mini-intifada" by Maronite troops also occurred in Jezzin, and Beirut condemned "hundreds" for their cooperation with Israel.[126] In 1999, Israel expelled 25 relatives of SLA militiamen from the security zone after the fighters deserted their post during Operation Grapes of Wrath.[127] Ultimately, salvaging and protecting its SLA partners became one of the primary reasons for the IDF to prolong its occupation.[128]

As a shift in Israeli public opinion became increasingly apparent, defections within SLA forces rapidly occurred. As noted by the head of Mabat, Akel Hesham, "Obviously, if your [Israeli] newspapers constantly talk about withdrawal, it will have an adverse effect on our soldiers and our ability to recruit agents . . . they say 'What will I get out of it?'"[129] Indeed, Israel had offered many SLA commanders amnesty, but the fate of foot soldiers was unknown.[130] Uncertainty over their future status led many SLA fighters to defect, yielding disastrous results. SLA intelligence officer Raja Ward defected to Lebanese authorities, for example, and handed them list of people working for Shabbak 501.[131] Lebanese authorities further targeted SLA members, and on February 11, 1999, the LAF arrested 20 people who were supposedly spying on Hezbollah.[132] SLA commander Lahad was also sentenced to death in absentia in a 1996 Lebanese military court.[133]

---

[125] Norton, 2000, p. 30.

[126] Hirst, 1999, p. 17.

[127] Sobelman, 1999.

[128] Herzog and Gazit, 2004, p. 391.

[129] Bergman, 1999b.

[130] ". . . and Its Crumbling Militia," 1998.

[131] Jones, 2001, pp. 1–26.

[132] "Jane's Intelligence Watch Report—Daily Update," 1999.

[133] Blanche, 1997.

In the wake of the IDF's unilateral withdrawal on September 15, 2000, the SLA swiftly collapsed. A military court sentenced 24 SLA fighters to terms of up to three years,[134] while 1,500 SLA fighters subsequently gave themselves up to the Lebanese government.[135] Although Hezbollah had long threatened repercussions for SLA soldiers,[136] Hezbollah Secretary General Hassan Nasrallah urged restraint, and most SLA fighters served a year in prison.[137] But some 6,500 SLA fighters and families were reportedly admitted into Israel, including Antoine Lahad.[138] By the time of the Israeli withdrawal, Israel had spent roughly $17 million to pay SLA fighters.[139]

The 1985–2000 period demonstrates the internal and external pressures that can cause local defense forces to disintegrate. The Home Guards' struggle with Shi'i militancy, coupled with the questionable loyalty of some of their leaders, led the program to crumble within roughly three years. Israeli attempts to build up the SLA through equipment improvements and economic incentives did temporarily lead the force to expand in numbers, however. Yet, this rapid expansion did not yield a more loyal or effective local defense force. When Israel attempted to capitalize on the force's potential as a conduit for intelligence on Hezbollah, the SLA proved unable or unwilling to do so. Furthermore, the force's ruthless actions isolated it from the Lebanese public.

Hezbollah's military strategy succeeded in separating the SLA from Lebanese communities and fostered uncertainty within SLA cadres. Hezbollah infiltration, assassinations, and information operations all undermined the SLA's capability and credibility with local communities. Thus, although the SLA's internal fissures and Israeli missteps contributed to the failure of local defense forces in southern

---

[134] "In Brief—Former SLA Militiamen Jailed," 2000.

[135] Blanford, 2000.

[136] Jaber, 1997; Blanford, 2000, p. 207.

[137] Cambanis, 2010, p. 263.

[138] Herzog and Gazit, 2004, p. 389.

[139] Barak and Sheffer, 2006. p. 254.

Lebanon, the components of Hezbollah's armed campaign played a significant role as well.

Conclusion and Assessment

Israel's failed experience with local defense forces points to a number of lessons. These lessons are particularly crucial as the United States employs Village Stability Operations and the Afghan Local Police program in rural Afghanistan.

The first lesson relates to achieving a necessary balance in recruitment incentives when establishing and expanding local defense forces. Throughout the Israeli experience, increased salaries did not render the local defense force more effective. Near the end of the 1990s, the salary of an SLA soldier nearly doubled that of his LAF counterpart. But, because SLA members were not necessarily motivated by a desire to stabilize their villages or rid them of PLO/Hezbollah influence, they were likely to do only the bare minimum necessary to continue drawing the financial perks. The use of these financial incentives to convince formerly pro-PLO power brokers to take positions as Home Guards commanders was further problematic, as their dedication to a stable, terrorist-free Lebanon was tenuous at best. Relying heavily on economic incentives and/or local strongmen to attract new recruits will not render a local defense force militarily effective or loyal to an occupying military.

Related to the first lesson, proper recruitment and vetting practices must be adopted to ensure the force will be able to establish and maintain local ties. Indeed, many of the SLA's recruits had been involved in previously established militias, which naturally undermined their local credibility and reputations. Further, personnel requirements led to abusive recruitment practices that jeopardized ties between the force and the local communities it was tasked to protect. Ultimately, recruitment needs for expanding local defense forces should not drive overly expedient recruiting practices or nonexistent vetting of fighters.

Next, the Israeli case demonstrates that it is crucial for local defense forces to reflect their immediate human terrain. The concept of the Home Guards program and the SLA's inclusion of Muslim foot soldiers to serve in their home villages were positive steps in this regard. But the SLA's command structure was still dominated by Christians, and the rank-and-file representation failed to attract the Muslim majority en masse. Occupying militaries thus need to be aware of the social aspects of their operating environments and ensure that they incorporate key confessional and social demographics into local defense forces.

Monitoring and accountability when building and partnering with a local defense force are also of key importance. The IDF often failed or refused to enforce restrictions on the abusive behavior of the SLA. In turn, the actions of the Home Guards and SLA forces alienated them from the local communities they were supposed to be defending. Although they do not always initially maintain robust ties to local political institutions, local defense forces still need to be held accountable for their actions.

Finally, the occupying force should delineate the desired end state of its local defense forces. Because it failed to navigate the complex trilateral relationship between the Lebanese government, the SLA, and its occupying forces, the IDF was essentially supporting an illegal force that was operating in spite of rather than in support of the host government. Although integrating these forces into the LAF eventually became an Israeli demand during negotiations, this was not articulated from the outset. More than irking the Lebanese government, this uncertain or undefined fate of SLA soldiers led to hesitance in joining, as well as eventual defections as an Israeli withdrawal became imminent. Hezbollah's messaging exploited this quite effectively. Local defense forces thus must be aware of and satisfied with how they will fare after their partnered occupation force leaves.

ill trained and its morale was abysmal. The economy was stagnating. Observers were shocked at the regime's ability to cling to power following the Soviet withdrawal, in large part because these observers missed the significance of three interrelated changes during the 1980–1987 period.[5]

First, the DRA attempted to rebuild the army and Ministry of Interior forces. When the Soviets intervened in 1979, desertions and combat had reduced the army to perhaps 50 percent of its total strength before the Herat mutiny, and Ministry of Interior forces had been reduced even more. The factional split and general discontent was so great that even as late as the autumn of 1981, Afghan army units were refusing to participate in military operations.[6] Some divisions were even more attenuated, with fewer than 1,000 men out of a complement of over 10,000. Whole brigades and battalions would sometimes defect to the insurgency or simply desert and go home.[7]

Over the seven years from 1980, however, substantial progress was made in expanding the security forces. A major reorganization in 1984–1985 standardized the force to a large extent.[8] By 1987, the army had nearly tripled in size and the Ministry of Interior had expanded nearly fivefold. Admittedly this was accomplished in part through the liberal use of press gangs, which led to questionable motivations of those so recruited.[9] Morale and factional problems remained, but the security forces were at least functional with substantial Soviet assistance. One Soviet officer who was an adviser from 1984 to 1987 noted that "[b]y the time I arrived in Afghanistan the Afghan army had been more or less fully reconstructed. Their officers were not bad and they were well armed."[10]

---

[5]   This discussion draws heavily on Giustozzi, 2000.

[6]   Giustozzi, 2000, pp. 67–68.

[7]   Braithwaite, 2011, p. 136.

[8]   Oliker, 2011, p. 39.

[9]   Braithwaite, 2011, pp. 137–138.

[10]   Braithwaite, 2011, p. 138.

The second change was the growing power and competence of the Afghan intelligence service, known as KhAD (for *Khadamat-e Etela'at-e Dawlati*, the State Information Agency). KhAD received enormous amounts of resources and training from the Soviet KGB. Its leader for most of this period was Mohammed Najibullah, who proved an able security chief. KhAD was incredibly ruthless and increasingly effective, penetrating mujahedin organizations and limiting urban subversion. Along with the KGB, it also worked to turn insurgent groups against their brethren.[11]

By 1986, KhAD had grown to nearly 60,000 personnel, including 30 mobile counterinsurgency groups with 12,000 members supported by 600 KGB advisers. That year, Najibullah ascended to the leadership of the country, as discussed more below. In addition, KhAD was upgraded to a full ministry, known as WAD (*Wizarat-e Amaniyyat-e Dawlati*, the Ministry for State Security).[12]

The growth and development of the army, the interior ministry, and KhAD would also be integral to the third major change, the creation of local defense forces, generally referred to as *militias*. These militias predated the DRA, as the Afghan kings had relied heavily on such local forces. However, by the end of the Daoud regime most of the older militias had been disbanded.[13]

Local Defense in the Democratic Republic of Afghanistan, 1980–1987

In the place of the older militias of the monarchy, the DRA created two basic types of militia force, which Giustozzi characterizes as "ideological" and "non-ideological." The former were tied heavily though not exclusively to PDPA cadres; the latter were frequently tribal forces or

---

[11] Braithwaite, 2011, pp. 138–139; Oliker, 2011, pp. 32–35; Eliot, 1990; and Andrew and Mitrokhin, 2005, pp. 408–409.

[12] Giustozzi, 2000, pp. 98–99 and 266.

[13] Giustozzi, 2000, pp. 198–199.

insurgent defectors. In practice, even the ideological militias seem to have been more nominally than actually ideological.

The two main forms of ideological militias were the *Sepayan-i Inqilab* ("Soldiers of the Revolution") and the Revolution Defense Groups, (the GDR). The former were principally urban, though they were often sent to rural areas, while the latter were drawn heavily from the villages. They were intended not only to provide local security but also to propagandize the population in favor of the revolution. Both were formed within the first year or so after the Soviet intervention but took time to grow in numbers, with the GDR becoming the dominant form of ideological militia.[14]

By 1987, there were some 33,000 members of the GDR, according to Giustozzi.[15] While primarily defensive, the GDR would also participate in some offensive or joint operation. In 1987, they were said to be responsible for "repelling 2,707 attacks against their villages, but they also carried out 281 independent operations (i.e., attacks against the mujahedin) and 209 joint ones."[16]

However, the numbers of GDR was insufficient to protect the bulk of the countryside. At the peak of their coverage, GDR were present in only "tens of villages" per province, covering at most only 6 percent of inhabited villages.[17] This was insufficient to provide the robust local defense needed to deny insurgent access to the population.

The Soviets and the DRA government therefore turned to nonideological local defense forces. Over the course of the period 1980–1987, these groups proliferated with some associated with the Ministry of Defense and the army, the Ministry of Interior, and KhAD, the intelligence service. Like the ideological militias, these nonideological militias began soon after the Soviet intervention but grew much more rapidly, which proved ultimately to be a mixed blessing for the DRA.

---

[14] Giustozzi, 2000, pp. 48–49.

[15] Giustozzi, 2000, p. 285.

[16] Giustozzi, 2000, p. 200.

[17] Giustozzi, 2000, p. 50.

One set of local defense forces of this type were the so-called "border militias." These were primarily tribal units, recruited when the border tribes proved reluctant to join the regular military. Initially organized under the Ministry of Tribes and Nationalities, there were 3,000 militia troops along the eastern border in 1980. By 1982, these militias were reorganized under the Ministry of Defense.[18]

The border militias were, as their name suggests, focused on interdicting insurgents along the border, mainly with Pakistan. They worked with the formal Border Troops, with mixed results. The border remained porous throughout the conflict, yet several of the border militias were highly committed to resisting the insurgency.

An early example of a committed border militia was led by Ismatullah Muslim and headquartered in Spin Boldak along the border with Pakistan in Kandahar province. Ismatullah was a former army officer and prominent member of the Achekzai tribe, which had traditionally been involved in smuggling. Ismatullah fled during the rule of Amin, forming an armed group in Pakistan. After a falling out with the mujahedin over stolen arms, he joined the government and was subsequently noted by many for his "high degree of activism against the mujahedin." By 1988, Ismatullah's militia had risen to somewhere between 4,000 and 10,000, with heavy weapons and armored vehicles.[19]

Another set of nonideological local defense forces were the regional or territorial forces. These were generally created to control a specific territory or region, though some served outside of their home region. As with the border militias, they drew heavily on tribal and ethnic ties. By 1987, there were nearly 90,000 men in these units.[20]

The most famous example of a regional force was led by Abdul Rashid Dostum from the area around Sherberghan in Jowzjan province. Dostum, an Uzbek former army officer, initially led a small mili-

---

[18] Giustozzi, 2000, pp. 200–201.

[19] Giustozzi, 2000, p. 206. Ismatullah's relatives in the Adozai clan of the Achekzai, including the current Kandahar provincial chief of police General Abdul Raziq, once again controlled Spin Boldak after the U.S. invasion in 2001. See Aikins, 2011; and Giustozzi, 2009.

[20] Giustozzi, 2000, p. 285.

tia protecting gas fields in the north. Over time his militia grew in size and capability until it was eventually converted into the 53rd Army Division. This division served as a mobile reserve for the DRA and was known as the most reliable and combative in the army. However, it fundamentally remained Dostum's force: Its members refused to wear army uniforms and owed loyalty to him, not to the state.[21]

The regional forces became increasingly important as the conflict continued. They began to take on ever more functions of police and other military units and even the functions of the government. This was driven in large part by the perceived effectiveness of the militia.[22]

As the war progressed, the government's focus shifted from winning the loyalty of both elites and the public and then creating militias to simply recruiting existing armed formations, particularly insurgents, and using them to control the population. This was a major distinction that showed the fading power of old elites and the rise of insurgent warlords. Money was critical to buying loyalty, with militiamen receiving double the pay of enlisted soldiers in 1987.[23]

Finally, even if the government could not buy the loyalty of local militias, it could often buy their neutrality. This made recruiting harder for the mujahedin, since they were forced to compete with these other loyalties.[24] Soviet soldiers, frequently working with KhAD officers, proved fairly effective in negotiating with locals. This was likely in part due to similar backgrounds—many Soviet soldiers had effectively been peasants, though admittedly on much better soil.[25]

---

[21] Giustozzi, 2000, pp. 222–223.

[22] Giustozzi, 2000, pp. 207–208

[23] Giustozzi, 2000, pp. 208–209 and 286.

[24] See Dunbar, 1987. This article also presents a good overview of the balance of forces late in this period.

[25] Braithwaite, 2011, pp. 181–183.

Soviet "Surge" and Withdrawal, 1987–1989

A major change came to the PDPA regime in 1986, when the head of KhAD, Najibullah, assumed power after the resignation of Babrak Karmal. This marked the ascendance of the security elite in KhAD over the Marxist scholars who had founded the PDPA. Najibullah proved to be more adept at using tribal and ethnic loyalties than Karmal, and he was also willing to make tactical concessions, such as calling for national reconciliation and offering cease-fires to the insurgents.

At the same time, changes in the Soviet leadership began the road to the end of the Afghan insurgency, as the old guard of Leonid Brezhnev and Yuri Andropov succumbed to age and infirmity in the early 1980s. Soon after coming to power in 1985, Soviet leader Mikhail Gorbachev seemed to have concluded that the conflict in Afghanistan was, if not unwinnable, not important enough to continue bearing both the physical and diplomatic costs it carried with it. However, Gorbachev's political position was not fully assured at this early point and he had a much broader agenda to lay the groundwork for than just withdrawal from Afghanistan. Many in the Soviet elite still felt that the Afghan conflict was either winnable outright or that an acceptable negotiated solution was possible if military pressure was increased.[26]

Rather than fight a major battle over Afghanistan policy at this early point, Gorbachev instead opted to allow significant escalation of the conflict in 1985–1986. Soviet troop numbers were not increased (except in the case of spetsnaz, or special forces, over a third of whom are alleged to have been deployed in Afghanistan during this period), but many other qualitative steps were taken. Activity along the border with Pakistan, including cross-border activity into the Pakistan sanctuary (first conducted in 1984) was increased. This took the form of spetsnaz air assault raids and aerial bombing. Massive bombing also had the effect of causing population migrations, denuding many areas of population and making it harder for the mujahedin to operate in them.[27]

---

[26] Kuperman, 1999.

[27] Dunbar, 1987.

However, this surge in effort was merely the prelude to with-drawal. At a November 1986 Politburo meeting, the Soviet leadership quietly changed its overall strategic goal in Afghanistan from maintaining a friendly socialist regime to ensuring a neutralist settlement and ending the war in two years or less. This strategic shift quickly led to diplomatic action. In December 1986, the Soviets informed Najibullah that Soviet troops would be withdrawn in 18 to 24 months. In July 1987, he was told that the withdrawal would be as early as a year later.[28]

The Soviets also began encouraging international negotiations that they had previously stalled. By early 1988, a settlement looked imminent, and Gorbachev offered to have all troops out by early 1989 if an accord could be signed by March. Obviously Najibullah was not happy with the prospect of a Soviet withdrawal, but he had little choice but to accept it and try to obtain the best settlement he could. Soviet promises of continued substantial aid made this prospect a little more palatable. The Geneva accords, signed in April 1988, called for a rapid Soviet withdrawal but allowed continued support to the DRA.

As Soviet troop levels began to fall in 1988, the Soviets continued to support their Afghan allies with extensive military aid. In particular they continued to provide massive air support to Afghan operations and to conduct cross-border aerial operations. The Soviets also provided the Afghan government with Scud B ballistic missiles, enabling the targeting of remote mujahedin base camps.[29]

During this period, the Najibullah regime was faced with the challenge of maintaining control of a factionalized party while at the same time seeking to expand the base of support for the regime. In May 1988, Najibullah named non-PDPA member Mohammed Hassan Sharq as prime minister and the Soviets threw considerable support into trying to make Sharq seem a viable noncommunist part of the regime. Cracks began to appear in the regime, as Najibullah thwarted a coup attempt in late 1988.[30]

---

[28] See Kuperman, 1999; and Westad, 1996/1997.

[29] Discussion of the Geneva Accords and subsequent Soviet aid is drawn from Cronin, 1989.

[30] Cronin, 1989.

By February 1989, the withdrawal of Soviet combat troops was complete. Najibullah and his factionalized regime were forced to stand alone against a well-armed insurgency operating from a foreign sanctuary. The demise of the PDPA and the DRA seemed at hand.

Najibullah's Tightrope, 1990–1991

The withdrawal of Soviet troops was widely expected to herald the end of the Najibullah regime within months if not weeks. Pakistan, in particular, was concerned with who would rule Afghanistan and wanted those most sympathetic to its cause to be well represented. In February 1989, as the last Soviet combat forces left the country, the insurgents formed the Afghan Interim Government (AIG), expecting a rapid victory.

The AIG decided to seize the strategically located town of Jalalabad, near the Pakistani border and on the road from the Khyber Pass to Kabul, as its capital. This attempt to move from guerrilla warfare to more conventional warfare was disastrous. SCUD missiles and Soviet-supported air power inflicted major losses on the insurgents once they massed for combat and after several months the siege was called off.[31]

Najibullah's response to the Soviet withdrawal was twofold. First, he took advantage of the freedom of maneuver the withdrawal had given him politically and purged his government of all non-PDPA personnel, such as Sharq. At the same time, he made a series of diplomatic overtures to the United States and the mujahedin, including offering the mujahedin local autonomy in exchange for an end to the war. Najibullah also began to play up both his Islamic faith and his Afghan nationalism, calling the mujahedin fanatics and bandits with no legitimacy.[32]

Even as he launched this combination of regime consolidation and diplomacy, Najibullah increasingly came to rely on the local mili-

---

[31] "Rebel Cabinet Holds 1st Session in Afghanistan," 1989; Weaver, 1989; Rupert, 1989.

[32] See Eliot, 1990.

tias to suppress the insurgency. Dostum's Uzbek militia, for example, continued to grow in size and equipment during this period, as did others, with the total number of local defense forces exceeding 170,000 (and even this may mask the total—Dostum technically commanded an army division though clearly it owed loyalty to him). Najibullah also continued to buy neutrality from other groups that he could not convert to his own side.[33]

Najibullah and the PDPA were sensitive to the loyalty of the militia and began taking steps to ensure that they stayed loyal. The regime worked to transform regional forces into national ones, but little progress was made. Loyal national units were also deployed to watch over regional forces.[34]

The situation in 1990 remained broadly similar to that of 1989, with some notable developments. Najibullah fought off another military coup attempt, subsequently shifting his cabinet somewhat to give the military more representation. The AIG also faced internal infighting, which Najibullah abetted as much as possible.[35]

The AIG also had fewer resources because U.S. support had dwindled after the Soviet withdrawal. Commanders were increasingly forced to turn to coerced resource extraction, otherwise known as banditry, and in some cases opium production.[36] The Afghan economy was so battered at this point that there was often little to extract, so external support became increasingly important. The Saudis and Pakistanis continued to provide support, so their influence was growing.

The AIG also had limited military success. Only Tarin Kot, the capital of sparsely populated Oruzgan province, fell to the insurgents in 1990. Attacks on the larger and more important provincial cities of Khost and Qalat failed.[37]

---

[33] Giustozzi, 2000, p. 285; Fineman, 1989; and Fineman, 1992a.

[34] Giusotzzi, 2000, pp. 219–220.

[35] Eliot, 1991.

[36] Tefft, 1990; Coll, 1990.

[37] Eliot, 1991.

As external support to the mujahedin tightened, the Soviets poured aid into the Najibullah regime at a rate estimated at over $300 million per month. Najibullah continued to use this aid to buy loyalty and neutrality from militias and to reward the security services, such as KhAD/WAD. In addition to buying support, he shifted his stance on the mujahedin somewhat, offering to create a national reconciliation government that would transition to elections; he even offered to give some security powers to the commission that would oversee the elections.[38]

At the beginning of 1991, the combination of ongoing disarray in the mujahedin and continued Soviet support for Najibullah resulted in further stalemate. However, major shifts would soon take place. First, in April a coordinated attack on the provincial capital of Khost, supported by Pakistan, was the first successful conventional operation by the mujahedin, using both tanks and artillery. The fall of Khost was heralded as the beginning of the end for Najibullah. However, the old divisions in the mujahedin had only been papered over. AIG members almost immediately fell out over the spoils of Khost, and were unable to secure Khost and prevent looting.[39]

Najibullah's response to the fall of Khost and rebel assaults on other cities was to continue attempting to refashion his regime to make it an acceptable partner in a transition government. He renamed the PDPA the "Homeland Party," and further embraced Islam while mounting more propaganda attacks that cast the mujahedin as fanatics under the sway of Saudi Wahhabi fundamentalism. The alliances with local militias remained vital to regime survival.[40]

The biggest changes in 1991 were again in terms of external support. Following the attempted August 1991 coup in Soviet Russia, the Soviet Union abruptly shifted its position on aid to Afghanistan as various hard-liners lost influence or were purged. At the same time, the United States was growing concerned about the factionalism and increasingly strident anti-American tone of many of the mujahedin

---

[38] Eliot, 1991.

[39] "Afghan Rebels Torn by New Quarrel," 1991.

[40] Tarzi, 1992.

restore order in Fallujah in April but suspened operations due to the level of destruction being inflicted on the city. An attempt was made to use an Iraqi unit cobbled together from various tribes to secure Fallujah, but this attempt was doomed from the start and Fallujah remained an insurgent stronghold through the summer of 2004.[1]

In November 2004, a second offensive, Operation PHANTOM FURY (also referred to by the Arabic AL FAJR "THE DAWN"), was launched to retake Fallujah. This massive force was opposed by heavily entrenched insurgents.[2] After more than a month of intense urban combat that devastated the city, the insurgents were forced out, having taken massive casualties. Insurgent operations shifted west along the WERV, operations increasingly dominated by Al Qaeda in Iraq (AQI).[3]

The nationalist insurgents and tribesmen who had previously supported the AQI began to have second thoughts beginning in early 2005. As AQI spread out through the province, many of the nationalists were beginning to consider participation in the political process, since the alternative seemed to be more battles like Fallujah to no gain. Tribesmen were increasingly angry as AQI took over their lucrative gray and black market activities, such as smuggling.[4]

The first open break between AQI and the Anbaris came around the town of Al Qaim in early 2005. Backed by the Albu Nimr tribe, the Albu Mahal tribe from the area formed a paramilitary unit known as the Hamza Brigade. Former governor Faisal al-Gaoud sought to establish a partnership between the Hamza Brigade and the Coalition but was initially unsuccessful. A May 2005 Coalition offensive, Operation MATADOR, damaged the city and killed members of the Hamza Brigade, ending attempts at cooperation for several months. In August, the Coalition began to support the Hamza Brigade with airpower,

---

[1]   See Malkasian, 2006.

[2]   See Malkasian, 2006; and Allam, 2004.

[3]   See Malkasian, 2006; Matthews, 2006; and West, 2005.

[4]   Long, 2008; and McCary, 2009.

but this was insufficient. By September 2005, the Hamza Brigade had been driven out of Al Qaim and was forced to retreat to Akashat.[5]

Around Ramadi, others began attempting to fight AQI. Sheikh Abdul Sattar Bezia al-Rishawi, a smuggler, gathered some tribal fighters, but they were crushed by the superior organization of AQI led in Ramadi by the ferocious Bassim Muhammad Hazim al-Fahadawi, commonly known by the *kunya* (an Arabic nickname derived from the name of the eldest child) Abu Khattab. Mohammed Mahmoud Latif, (MML) and other nationalists also decided to turn against AQI at some point during mid- to late 2005. These nationalists, operating under a new umbrella organization called the Anbar People's Council (APC), fought against AQI and also sought to help the Coalition protect the elections for the new national government in December 2005.[6]

AQI's response to the APC was ruthless and devastating. In February 2006, under the direction of Abu Khattab, they assassinated key personnel, including the well-respected Sheikh Nassir al-Fahadawi, the leader of both Abu Khattab's and MML's tribe. Others were intimidated and cowed by these actions. MML himself was a target and apparently fled. Other anti-AQI nationalists, possibly including remnants of the APC, formed the Anbar Revolutionaries (often known by its Arabic acronym TAA) at about the same time. TAA used a combination of targeted killings and propaganda, such as graffiti and leaflets, in a campaign intended to weaken and discredit AQI. While this clandestine organization had some success with assassinations of AQI targets, including Abu Khattab, it was simply not sufficient to reverse AQI's growing ascendancy.[7]

Not everything was going AQI's way, however. In November 2005, Faisal al-Gaoud and others successfully arranged a major partnership between the Hamza Brigade and the Coalition. This partnership led to the launch of a major offensive around Al Qaim called

---

[5] Nickmeyer and Finer, 2005; Malkasian, 2007a, and 2007b.

[6] See Devlin, 2006; "AQI Situation Report," undated; Harnden, 2005; and Multinational Force–Iraq, 2006.

[7] See Devlin, 2006; "AQI Situation Report," undated; Multinational Force–Iraq, 2006; "Iraqi Rebels Turn on Qaeda in Western City," 2006; and Finer and Nickmeyer, 2005.

Operation STEEL CURTAIN, which eventually drove AQI out and secured the town.[8] The Hamza Brigade was renamed the Desert Protectors and began to work closely with U.S. special operations forces.[9]

The success around Al Qaim remained an isolated success until Sheikh Sattar, Faisal al-Gaoud, Hamid Farhan al-Heiss (from the Albu Thiyab tribe), Sheikh Ali Hatim al-Assafi, and other tribal leaders around Ramadi once again sought to oppose AQI. Hamid Heiss and Ali Hatim formed the Anbar Salvation Council (ASC), which may have overlapped in membership with TAA. Sheikh Sattar formed the Anbar (later Iraqi) Awakening (known by its Arabic acronym SAA, later SAI) and it also may have overlapped with TAA. The two organizations joined together in fighting AQI and at this point (mid-2006) were under the overall guidance of Sattar, who had a flair for the dramatic and a strong personality.[10]

Under Sattar, the two organizations began cooperating with Coalition forces against AQI, which at this time dominated much of Ramadi. The full story of how this cooperation emerged remains somewhat opaque because it involved Marine battalions, an Army brigade command, special operations forces, and, it seems likely, CIA officers.[11] Yet however it happened, ASC and SAA began, with U.S. assistance, to enroll their memberships in the Iraqi Police, tying them into the formal state security apparatus. Those that did not become uniformed police were incorporated into police auxiliary formations known as Emergency Response Units (ERUs) or Provincial Security Forces (PSFs).

---

[8]   See Malkasian, 2007b; and Anderson, 2005.

[9]   Searle, 2008; Tyson, 2006.

[10] McCary, 2009; Malkasian, 2007a; Jaffe, 2007; Kukis, 2006.

[11] On Marine and Army involvement, see, among others, McWilliams and Wheeler, 2009; and Russell, 2011. On special operations forces, see Searle, 2008; Tyson, 2006; and Couch, 2008. On CIA involvement, see Searle, 2008; Urban, 2010; and Manning, 2008. Manning cites remarks by former CIA director Michael Hayden at the Air Force Association's annual conference: "[T]he CIA is working closely with the military in places such as Iraq's Anbar province, where American troops have fought Sunni insurgents. That experience helped CIA officers develop a strategy to engage Sunni tribal leaders, which Hayden said has contributed to a recent drop in violence in Iraq."

Even as this cooperation to create local security developed around Ramadi, the situation was so dire across Anbar that an August 2006 Marine Corps intelligence assessment deemed that social order had all but collapsed and AQI held sway over most of what was left.[12] However, as with the Desert Protectors in Al Qaim, the combination of Coalition firepower and money with the tribal leaders' local knowledge rapidly began to reverse the situation in Ramadi. SAI affiliates and copycats began to appear in other parts of the province. Around the Haditha Triad, Coalition forces partnered principally with members of Albu Jughayfi; in Karmah it was with local tribesmen led by the Albu Jumayli.[13]

Managing the relations between these tribes could be challenging for Coalition forces. For example, the U.S. support to local defense conducted by the Abu Mahal tribe around Al Qaim empowered the tribe over its rivals the Abu Karbul and the Albu Salman. This pushed those later tribes toward AQI as they felt disadvantaged by the U.S. efforts with the Abu Mahal. U.S. military personnel in the region had to work assiduously to limit this intertribal rivalry.[14]

The same phenomenon was true of the Albu Jughayfi around Haditha. The dominance of the Jughayfi in the local defense forces established with U.S. assistance alienated other tribes in the area, who felt the Jughayfi targeted them regardless of whether they were insurgents or not. This again required careful management to prevent exploitation by the insurgency.[15] Unfortunately by March 2012 the insurgency may have been able to exploit this rift, as insurgents posing as police assassinated the leader of the Haditha local defense, Colonel Mohammed Shafir, a Jughayfi leader known widely to the Americans as "Sheikh Mo."[16]

---

[12] Devlin, 2006.

[13] Armstrong, 2008; author observations, Anbar, May–August 2008.

[14] Perry, 2008; author observations, Fallujah, April–August 2008.

[15] Armstrong, 2008; author conversations and observations in Anbar, November 2007 and April–August 2008.

[16] Healy, 2012.

The Army approach was clearly very hands-off, as it apparently left most hiring decisions to the locals. The upside of this approach was that it enabled very rapid expansion of the numbers of these local defense forces. By early 2009 there were roughly 95,000 SOI, about half of whom were in Baghdad.[26] In contrast, there were only a few thousand SOI in Anbar province, concentrated in the extreme east of the province along the border with Baghdad.[27]

An extensive explanation of the difference between the evolution of the Anbar Awakening and the subsequent creation of SOI is beyond the scope of this monograph. However, at least three related factors probably explain the divergence. First, the U.S. Army and the U.S. Marine Corps have very different organizational cultures, with the latter having a much greater historical affinity for local defense forces.[28] Second, there was apparently substantially greater direct involvement of CIA and special operations personnel in the Anbar Awakening than the creation of the SOI. Finally, while the Anbar Awakening was the result of a series of local initiatives, and therefore had little pressure to rapidly expand, the SOI program did face pressure to grow rapidly as it came to be viewed as a major element of the counterinsurgency effort. This in turn meant speed was of the essence, which argued against taking time to incorporate the SOIs into the formal state security apparatus.

Moreover, the relationship between government of Iraq security forces, particularly the Iraqi army, and the SOIs was not always harmonious. For example, in eastern Anbar (Zaidon/Nasser wa Salaam) and Baghdad's Abu Ghraib neighborhood, Sons of Iraq leaders came into

---

[26] Nordland and Rubin, 2009; and interviews with Force Strategic Engagement Cell (FSEC) personnel, Baghdad, December 2009. This and other interviews noted below in 2009–2010 were conducted by the author on behalf of the International Crisis Group. See International Crisis Group, 2010. See also Lynch, 2011; and Marten, 2012.

[27] Author interviews, Fallujah, August 2008.

[28] See Long, 2010.

conflict with Iraqi Army units. Conflicts such as these required mediation by U.S. forces.[29] This further argued against trying to incorporate the SOI into the state apparatus.

However, despite these issues the Sons of Iraq contributed to the success of counterinsurgency across Iraq. In 2008 testimony to the Senate Armed Services Committee, MNF-I commander Gen. Petraeus, noted:

> Since the first Sunni "Awakening" in late 2006, Sunni communities in Iraq increasingly have rejected AQI's indiscriminate violence and extremist ideology. These communities also recognized that they could not share in Iraq's bounty if they didn't participate in the political arena. Over time, Awakenings have prompted tens of thousands of Iraqis—some, former insurgents—to contribute to local security as so-called "Sons of Iraq.". . . The emergence of Iraqi volunteers helping to secure their local communities has been an important development . . . there are now over 91,000 Sons of Iraq—Shia as well as Sunni—under contract to help Coalition and Iraqi Forces protect their neighborhoods and secure infrastructure and roads. These volunteers have contributed significantly in various areas, and the savings in vehicles not lost because of reduced violence—not to mention the priceless lives saved—have far outweighed the cost of their monthly contracts.[30]

Reintegrating the Sons of Iraq, 2008–2009

The Sons of Iraq program was then transitioned to the government of Iraq in late 2008 and early 2009. The plan moving forward from that transition was to integrate about 20 percent of the fighters into the regular Iraqi security forces while the remainder would receive

---

[29] Author observations, Fallujah, April–August 2008.

[30] Petraeus, 2008.

a job in some other government ministry. In the meantime, the government of Iraq would continue to pay the Sons of Iraq salaries.[31]

In practice, this reintegration plan and the overall relationship between the government and the SOI has been problematic. The government of Iraq had always been skeptical of the program, given the background of its members. They were often regarded as thugs at best and Sunni terrorists at worst. The SOI often did not hold the government in much higher regard.[32]

Over the course of 2010, Sons of Iraq around Baghdad were transitioned into either Iraqi security forces or other ministry jobs. Those were not transitioned continued to work as Sons of Iraq, receiving paychecks from the government. Reports of how well this transition proceeded vary widely. Iraqi government officials viewed it as relatively successful while former Sons of Iraq leaders felt it had been problematic.[33]

According to U.S. personnel in the FSEC, which has been involved extensively in the program, the truth is somewhere in between. There were initial problems in paying SOI salaries in March through May 2009, but by October 2009, after the salaries were made a line item in the budget of the Implementation and Follow-Up Committee for National Reconciliation, the problems had mostly been resolved and payments had been caught up. However, since October 2009, payments had "fallen behind a little."[34]

The transition of Sons of Iraq around Baghdad has been ongoing, though not without problems. By late August 2009, roughly 3,300 Sons of Iraq had been transitioned into government ministry jobs.[35] From August to December 2009, a total of roughly 23,000 Sons of Iraq were transitioned into government ministry jobs, though

---

[31] Nordland and Rubin, 2009.

[32] Nordland and Rubin, 2009; Mulrine, 2009.

[33] Interviews with government of Iraq and Sons of Iraq leaders, Baghdad, December 2009.

[34] Interviews with FSEC personnel, Baghdad, December 2009.

[35] Olsen, 2009.

events like the ministry bombings in August and October 2009 slowed the pace.[36]

There were also arguments about transitioning Sons of Iraq into Iraqi security forces positions at a time when both the Ministry of Defense and Ministry of Interior had a hiring freeze in place. However, the disputes were resolved, and between 7,000 and 13,000 SOI in Baghdad were transitioned into Iraqi security forces in 2009. But it was anticipated that the SOI would remain in parts of Baghdad through at least March 2010.[37] As of December 2010, the government of Iraq reported that it had transitioned nearly 40,000 (almost half the total number of SOI), but these were mostly in Baghdad.[38]

This would seem to be a relatively successful transition. However, many Sons of Iraq who have been transitioned into government ministry jobs have been unhappy in their new positions, which are often menial and far from their home neighborhoods. It was certainly viewed as a loss of status to go from carrying a weapon in defense of one's neighborhood to sweeping up at a ministry across town. Some Sons of Iraq viewed this as a sign of the government's disregard for their well-being. To be fair, few of the Sons of Iraq were particularly well educated so it would not have been possible in many cases to give them a higher-status job in a ministry.[39]

In addition to concerns over the transition of individual rank-and-file Sons of Iraq, there have been concerns about the treatment of SOI leaders. These leaders have been targeted extensively in a campaign of assassination over the past several years, with 212 being killed

---

[36] Interview with FSEC personnel, Baghdad, December 2009.

[37] Comments by Major General John Johnson, August 27, 2009; interview with General Nasir Abadi, Baghdad, December 2009; interview with FSEC personnel, Baghdad, December 2009. The discrepancy in numbers may reflect different timing or different interpretations of what counted as transitioned.

[38] Office of the Special Inspector General for Iraq Reconstruction, 2011, p. 17.

[39] Interview with U.S. government analysts, Washington, D.C., November 2009; interview with U.S. government analyst, Baghdad, December 2009; interview with FSEC personnel, Baghdad, December 2009.

In most of the other cases, expansion was slow at first but accelerated over the course of the conflict. In some cases, there was reasonably close oversight (Oman); in others, much less so (Afghanistan); in Algeria and Indochina, it was mixed.

Oversight has the added bonus of mitigating the risk of unintended use of local defense forces. In El Salvador, the lack of oversight led to real concerns that Civil Defense units were acting as death squads. Similarly, the lack of close oversight exacerbated Iraqi government concerns about criminal activity and extrajudicial killing by the Sons of Iraq.

A third technique is to create a local defense force using actors that are on relatively good terms with the national government. The Fighting Fathers in South Vietnam is a clear example of this, as the Catholic-dominated government of President Ngo Dinh Diem had little concern about armed Catholics led by priests. The same was true of some leaders of the Anbar Awakening in Iraq, such as Hamid Heiss and Ali Hatem, who possessed or rapidly developed ties to politicians in Baghdad.

Yet this technique is often self-limiting—if the government were already on good terms with large segments of the population, it would rarely need substantial U.S. assistance in creating local defense. This means that local defense units with which the government is inherently on good terms are frequently drawn from minorities (e.g. ethnic, tribal, or religious) that will have a limited strategic effect. Indeed, this is true of any program that relies on minorities, whether pro- or anti-government. As CIA case officer and historian Thomas Ahern notes of CIDG and Fighting Fathers, both used minorities effectively, yet "[t]he programs . . . left the major issue, the loyalties of the Buddhist-Confucian majority, still to be confronted."[6] External actors are also in a better position to recruit groups *not* on good terms with the central government because these groups generally have clear grievances that can be addressed in exchange for counterinsurgency support, as was the case of the Rhade tribe in Vietnam. This, however, is likely to create additional tensions with the central government if the

---

[6]   Ahern, 2001, p. 78.

government is still not ready to make such compromises. In addition to managing the trilateral relationship between the United States, the host nation's government, and local actors, the relationship between local actors must often be managed as well. Local actors will have their own particular interests and grudges, and efforts to create local defense creates opportunities for some actors to gain at the expense of others, as happened with the tribes around Al Qaim in Iraq.

Yet as at the national level, U.S. leverage over local actors is frequently limited. U.S. actions did not cause the Awakening in Iraq. Instead, various local tribes found it in their interest to turn against AQI beginning in 2005, which then made an alliance with the United States possible. There is no evidence that it would have been possible had the United States sought such an alliance earlier; indeed, an attempt to secure Fallujah with local defenders failed abjectly in early 2004. The same is true of CIDG, where U.S. support came after a willingness to fight against insurgents. Therefore, an important lesson is to be prepared to take advantage of shifts in local actors' interests and to try to incentivize shifts where possible, but to avoid attempting to create local defense forces where communities have no interest in them.

Lesson Two: Capitalize on Intelligence Collection

The second lesson from the historical cases is that the value of local defenders comes primarily, though not exclusively, from their ability to provide intelligence rather than from their efficacy as combat forces. Although the combat effectiveness of the PFs in CAP improved with Marine tutelage, they were still fundamentally part-time paramilitaries, not professional combat soldiers. However, they had local knowledge of both society and geography that made them effective at gathering intelligence. The same was true of CIDG.

Iraqis familiar with the Sons of Iraq had similar feelings about their value, arguing it was intelligence that made them indispensable rather than their martial prowess. In contrast, intelligence from the Civil Defense in El Salvador was not well integrated with the overall military effort, limiting the utility of even those Civil Defense units that were competent. The French had similar success with GCMA and *commandos de chasse* in Indochina and Algeria.

The synergy of local defense force intelligence and conventional military capability presents insurgents with a nearly intractable dilemma. If the insurgency remains highly dispersed, it can avoid U.S. firepower but becomes vulnerable to defeat in detail as local defense forces, armed with good intelligence on their villages or neighborhoods, pick them off one by one. Yet if the insurgents mass to take advantage of the military weakness of local defense forces, they become lucrative targets for U.S. firepower.

The Battle of Donkey Island in Iraq demonstrates the mechanism of this dilemma. Similarly, the firqat and the harkis worked best in conjunction with regular forces. The "flying finger" technique in Oman made excellent use of firqat intelligence as did operations alongside SAF. Only half of the harkis were ever armed with military weapons, so it was vital they coordinate with other French military forces.

However, in some cases well-armed local defense units with excellent motivation and leadership can be effective in conventional warfare. The regional forces in Afghanistan, along with the GCMA and *commandos de chasse* in Indochina and Algeria, were highly effective in many instances of at least semi-conventional combat. However, they appear to be more the exception than the rule, in part because using these forces far from their homes (which conventional operations frequently entail) can create problems with desertion—as seen in Vietnam, Indochina, and Algeria.

A corollary to this lesson is that local defense is not static defense. Each of the successful local defense efforts examined in this study placed a premium on patrolling, often on foot. Patrolling not only enables intelligence collection on the enemy, it also allows for better understanding of the local dynamics of the conflict that is so crucial to successful management of political relationships. Firqat in Oman, for example, conducted vigorous patrols and intelligence collection.

A final caveat, related to the earlier point about managing local grudges and grievances, is that intelligence provided by local defense forces may be colored by these rivalries. In civil wars, political scientist Stathis Kalyvas compellingly demonstrates much of the intelligence provided by collaborators with either side is driven by those seeking to settle scores by denouncing local rivals.[7] This pattern seems to hold true in at least some of the cases examined here. In Iraq, for example, there were several instances, such as with the Albu Jughayfi in Anbar, in which those detained by U.S. forces based on intelligence provided by local defense forces turned out to be tribal or personal rivals of those providing the intelligence.[8]

Lesson Three: Beware of Local History

A third lesson concerns the long shadow of history. The importance of local history and politics (down to the village and neighborhood level) is apparent in each of the cases examined. In Vietnam, the historical treatment of ethnic and religious minorities, combined with specific dynamics at Buon Enao, made it an ideal place to launch a local defense program. Only a careful effort by "Mr. Dave" and "Dr. Paul" to canvass the Montagnard areas enabled its selection and the program's subsequent, if transient, success. Similarly, CIA knowledge of the "Fighting Fathers" from earlier programs enabled an equivalent understanding.

The Marines were able, over time, to develop an understanding of local politics in their areas of operations. Indeed, officers like Lt. Ek were selected to develop CAP because they were attuned to such nuances. At all levels, Marine personnel reached out to PF platoons, seeking to find those who would be amenable to partnership and capable of improving with training. Absent this knowledge, successes such as those at Binh Nghia would have been much more difficult. In Iraq, U.S. personnel developed over time the same detailed understanding of local dynamics that emerged in South Vietnam.

In El Salvador, the history of ORDEN cast a long shadow over local defense in many communities. Where the community's experience was not terrible, community support for Civil Defense was forthcoming and the program succeeded. Where ORDEN abuses led to hostility, the program foundered. The limited U.S. presence in El Salvador prevented the kind of detailed understanding that CIA, Special

---

[7] See Kalyvas, 2006, especially pp. 330–376.

[8] Author conversations and observations in Iraq, September–November 2007.

stantially longer than anticipated and faces many more difficulties. In Iraq, the transition of the SOI has taken much longer and experienced more problems than originally envisioned. Similarly the transitioning of CIDG units was slow and problematic in South Vietnam.

Conversely, unsuccessful transition can occur much more rapidly than anticipated. The collapse of the Afghan militia system when money ran out took place literally within a month, far faster than anyone, including the insurgency, anticipated. The harkis and the SLA also experienced massive dislocation and/or rapid collapse once it was clear that they had no future.

The problem of transition seems particularly pressing when economics (i.e., pay) is the prime motivator for local defense. In both Afghanistan and southern Lebanon this was a prime motivator that led to rapid and failed transition as the money ran out. Economic incentives are therefore a weak foundation for local security.

In contrast, local defense forces with strong ties to the community performed well with little or no pay. None of the local defense forces in South Vietnam were particularly well paid but they fought very well in some cases. Even in El Salvador, where local defense was not well established, Civil Defense units that had strong community ties frequently performed well despite little pay or equipment.

In general, this lesson highlights the fact that local defense forces, while often vital to counterinsurgency, are more difficult to manage than they might seem to be on the surface. While they may be a cheap and/or effective means to combat insurgency, they can take on a life of their own (or, to be more precise, they can become an integral part of the political economy). Nowhere is this more clear than Oman, where the firqat continue to exist more than three decades after the end of the insurgency, albeit in a greatly attenuated form. In some cases, the only viable transition may simply be to maintain the local defense force on the payroll.

Here again, the relationship between local defense forces and the central government is of critical importance. High levels of mistrust—including local defense forces' fear of being prosecuted, as was the case for the SOI—may result in a difficult and sometimes unsuccessful reintegration process, with former combatants keeping their arms or remaining de facto mobilized. An extreme case is Algeria, where the new central government had no intention to promote reconciliation with those who had supported the French colonial power. Failure to anticipate this outcome and to support local defense forces in this transition resulted in dramatic and long-lasting consequences for all involved.

Lesson Seven: Avoid Insurgent Strongholds

A seventh lesson is the importance of building local defense in areas where the insurgency has been militarily weakened rather than going directly for strongholds. This was most dramatically demonstrated with the APC, where the weakened insurgency after Tet was unable to mount a challenge to the rapid expansion and creation of hundreds of local defense formations in areas previously contested. Exploiting such weakness is critical to preventing the regeneration of a durable insurgency.

Yet insurgency need not be weakened by the counterinsurgents' direct military action alone. Defections from insurgent ranks or infighting can be a powerful tool for weakening the insurgency. In Oman, the defection by the men who would make up the firqat provided this needed weakening. Similar patterns can be seen in Algeria, Iraq, and Afghanistan, with defectors or disgruntled insurgents not only forming the nucleus of local defense in some cases but also weakening the insurgency sufficiently to provide an opening for the creation of local defense.

However, even a militarily weakened insurgency can challenge the establishment of local defense. In western Iraq in 2005, the lack of coordination between various elements of the U.S. government and the nascent movement against AQI delayed the establishment of effective local defense for months despite AQI being attacked by U.S. special operations, U.S. conventional forces, and tribal militias.

Other Lessons

In addition to the broader lessons that run through all or many of the cases, there are additional lessons to be learned from a few of the cases.

These lessons may not be as broadly applicable but are still potentially useful. This section briefly highlights these lessons.

First, the utility to local defense of insurgent mistakes that alienate a population was evident in Oman and Iraq particularly. The overreach in goals and actions of PFLOAG and AQI created the conditions for local defense. The phenomenon of insurgent mistakes is fairly common but requires the counterinsurgent to exercise patience and to try to create opportunities for the insurgents to overreach.[9] In Oman, the reforms of Sultan Qaboos directly created the opportunity for PFLOAG overrreach, while in Iraq the U.S. role in creating the opportunity was much more oblique. Regardless of the source of the insurgent mistake, efforts to create local defense in either country before these mistakes had been made were doomed. Counterinsurgents must be prepared to wait rather than try to force the issue.

Second, defectors from the insurgency who immediately join local defense forces can be extraordinarily useful. Such defection has multiple benefits: It provides a wealth of very current intelligence, allows the defectors to protect themselves from reprisal, and demonstrates the potential for reintegration into the political order. This is evident in Iraq, Algeria, Oman, and Indochina to some degree.

However, the possibility of redefection or infiltration of the local defense force is very real. Such an "insider threat" can be damaging to the counterinsurgency in multiple ways. It can sow distrust between the parties of the trilateral relationship; compromise intelligence and operations; and ruin the reputation of the local defense force with the population. On net, it seems that allowing defectors into the local defense force is positive but requires unusually high levels of assessment, vetting, and oversight of the newly defected.

Third, perceptions of different treatment or rivalry between local defense forces and regular security forces can create serious problems. Differences in pay, discipline, ethnicity, and the like can all create friction. This was demonstrated in Indochina, Oman, and Iraq and reduced operational efficacy in some cases. While it is not necessary for the local defense force and the regular security forces to be treated

---

[9]   On this phenomenon generally, see Krause, 2009.

identically, such matters as differences in pay must be clearly explained (for example, local defenders may be paid less because they do not have to deploy across the country).

Fourth, in the Lebanon and Algeria cases, defections from the local defense forces began to increase as withdrawal of the third party counterinsurgent neared. Many of these deserters took their arms with them. This was likely in part because they feared (rightly as it turned out) that they would be "sold out" in the peace agreement. There are some who believe a similar phenomenon occurred in Iraq, but the evidence is not available to make a clear judgment.

Regardless, it is worth noting this phenomenon and taking steps to prevent it. One method would be to provide a credible reassurance to members of the local defense force that they will be protected after withdrawal. Alternatively, the local defense force must be demobilized prior to imminent withdrawal. Neither of these options is likely to be easy, but the Soviets in Afghanistan demonstrated that it can be done (the Soviets chose essentially the first option, combined with extensive economic and military support).

Fifth, several cases show the importance of employing local defense forces close to their region of origin. In the case of Indochina, it prevented defections and reduced the risks that these forces would commit exactions against local populations. In El Salvador, community support to the local defense forces proved of key importance. In Algeria, proximity resulted in better intelligence and avoided mixing in a same unit rival groups and tribes. However, it also increased risks of retaliation by the insurgents against the families of local defense forces members.

Local Defense in Afghanistan After 2008

In March 2009, U.S. units in conjunction with the Afghan Ministry of the Interior initiated the Afghan Public Protection Program in Wardak province. This was the first attempt to create a local defense force in Afghanistan since the disbanding of the Afghan Auxiliary Police in 2008. The Auxiliary Police, essentially an attempt to put a veneer of government authority on various militias, had proved more trouble than it was worth, providing little security. The Afghan Public Protection Program sought to bring much higher levels of training and oversight to local defense. However, the process was too cumbersome for some in the U.S. special operations community.[10]

In June 2009, U.S. special operations forces began exploring other opportunities to create local defense forces. This new program was initially called the Community Defense Initiative, with the first efforts in Day Kundi, Herat, Nangarhar, and Paktiya established between August and November 2009. This program differed from the Afghan Public Protection Program in that while both sought to create stability and local defense forces at the village level, the new program did not involve the Ministry of Interior. Instead it sought to work directly with village level leadership who had decided to resist insurgent influence by placing a special operations team in a village to support that local leadership. In December 2009, the program was renamed the Local Defense Initiative.

Over the next year, the Local Defense Initiative expanded but encountered resistance from both the U.S. embassy and the Afghan government. Both were concerned that the program created the potential for the resurrection of predatory militias. In March 2010, the U.S. special operations role in the program was renamed Village Stability Operations, reflecting the idea that the goal of the program was more than just the creation of local defense forces but included strengthening the local and district government and economy. In mid-2010, Coalition and Afghan leadership agreed to bring the local defense force under the Ministry of Interior, so in August President Karzai signed a decree establishing the Afghan Local Police (ALP).

The result of this evolution is that as of August 2011 there are two separate but interrelated programs focused on village-level stability and local defense in Afghanistan. Village Stability Operations are con-

---

[10] This discussion of local defense in Afghanistan draws heavily on Madden, 2011; and the author's field research and experience with the local defense effort in June 2010, January 2011, and June–August 2011; also Lefèvre, 2010; Jones and Munoz, 2010; Islamic Republic of Afghanistan Ministry of Interior, 2011a, 2011b.

ducted by U.S.-led Coalition forces (principally but not exclusively special operations), while the ALP are a formal component of the Afghan police under the Ministry of Interior.

Numbering more than 7,000 in 43 districts in August 2011, the ALP have defensive responsibilities and are restricted to operating in their home districts (few operate outside their home village).[11] A unit is formed when a community's elders express an interest in the ALP and subsequently meet with representatives of the Afghan government, including the Ministry of Interior, the Independent Directorate for Local Governance, and representatives of the U.S.-led Coalition at a validation *shura*. Once the community's request is validated by the shura, the Ministry of Interior's Directorate of Local Police establishes a formal *tashkil* (manning authorization) for a district. This tashkil is generally limited to 300 per district, which is then divided up among different villages in the district. The units are equipped by the Ministry of Interior with U.S. support.

Members of the unit are volunteers from the community between the ages of 18 and 45 who sign a one-year contract. They are nominated by a village shura and then vetted by the Ministry of Interior with support from the National Directorate of Security (the Afghan internal security intelligence organization). Members work part-time and are paid approximately 60 percent of basic police salary. They are permitted to work at other jobs provided that the job does not abuse their position and is in accordance with the Afghan Police Law. The ALP are subject to all the same restrictions as the Afghan National Police, including on the use of force. They have the ability to temporarily detain suspects but cannot formally arrest them. Instead they turn detained suspects over to the Afghan National Police for arrest.

The ALP are subject to extensive control and oversight.Units are commanded by a Deputy District Chief of Police, who is an Afghan National Police officer appointed by the District Chief of Police. The units are also responsible to the village shura that sponsored them. ALP units are typically partnered with and mentored by U.S. and/or

---

[11] NATO Training Mission–Afghanistan, 2011. Note that there are districts that have an approved ALP *tashkil* that as of August 2011 had no ALP personnel.

Afghan forces that provide additional oversight. Typically these are special operations forces that are conducting village stability operations. This oversight by both Afghan and U.S. forces ensures that any abuses by the ALP can be quickly corrected by firing offenders or potentially prosecuting them for serious offenses.

Conclusion: The Application of Lessons to Afghan Local Police

As the foregoing indicates, U.S. special operations forces are applying most of the lessons learned from the case studies presented here. While the program is at least implicitly (and some would say explicitly) intended to outflank issues with the central government of Afghanistan, strenuous efforts have been made to manage the trilateral relationship. By transforming the Local Defense Initiative into village stability operations, U.S. special operations have substantially mitigated (though not eliminated) central government concerns about the program. The combination of Afghan and U.S. oversight likewise mitigates the potential for abuse.

Ongoing high-level engagements between U.S. and Afghan leaders have kept the program on track even as the numbers of Afghan Local Police has rapidly expanded. The total force strength averaged a monthly increase of over 13 percent from February to August 2011, a growth rate that will double the force roughly every six months if sustained, though there is currently a goal/limit of 30,000.[12] However, as with Operation SWITCHBACK, continual rapid expansion could begin to weaken the current relative harmony between U.S. special operations forces, local actors, and the Afghan government.

In terms of appropriate tactical employment of the ALP, U.S. special operations forces seem to be following the lessons learned. While there is a frequent use of the ALP as checkpoint security, this is often combined with patrolling and intelligence collection. One special operations team that one of the authors visited in July 2011 was working

---

[12] NATO Training Mission–Afghanistan, 2011.

with its ALP partner unit to establish a schedule of multiple night patrols around the village in order to counter insurgent intimidation and "night letters" (threats posted on people's doors under cover of night).[13] Elsewhere, the ALP are partnering with Afghan National Police to conduct patrols even without special operations forces.[14]

The quality of ALP units, and therefore their patrolling and intelligence collection, varies across Afghanistan. Thus, the mere fact that patrols take place is not indicative of effectiveness. The same is true of intelligence collection efforts. However, so far as the authors can ascertain, the ALP have not been used as conventional forces, as happened with CIDG strike forces, nor are they consigned almost solely to static checkpoints as with Civil Defense in El Salvador.

U.S. special operations forces have remained highly cognizant of the importance of history to perceptions of local defense forces in Afghanistan. The reputation of militias in Afghanistan since the 1990s has been very poor and so special operations forces have made strenuous (if not always successful) efforts to dissociate the Afghan Local Police from militias. They have repeatedly emphasized the importance of the Ministry of Interior as the national government partner and the local shura, district governor, and district chief of police as the local partners.

In terms of development, the village stability operations conducted by special operations forces emphasize community decisionmaking to prioritize both Coalition and Afghan government funds. These funds generally go for small infrastructure projects, such as wells and irrigation. At the same time, the special operations teams also seek to bring in funding from outside agencies, such as USAID, for larger development projects such as road construction. The system is not perfect, but it does indicate that U.S. special operations forces are cognizant of the lessons learned from previous local defense efforts.

Cooperation with other agencies remains somewhat opaque. It has been reported in the press and by nongovernmental organizations that the Afghan National Directorate of Security (NDS) and other agencies

---

[13] Author field notes in Kandahar province, July 2011. For security reasons the specific team location is omitted.

[14] Combined Joint Special Operations Task Force Afghanistan, 2011.

Akehurst, John, *We Won a War: The Campaign in Oman 1965–1975,* Salisbury, UK: Michael Russell, 1982.

al-Askari, Mohammed, "Iraqi Ministry of Defense Operational Update, June 15," *Operation New Dawn,* Official Website of United States Forces—Iraq, June 15, 2008. As of July 11, 2012:
http://www.globalsecurity.org/wmd/library/news/iraq/2008/06/iraq-080615-mnfi-b01.htm

"'al-Haras al-Watani fi Bara'shit Fajara Manzilayn" ("The Home Guards in Barashit Exploded Two Houses"), *al-Nahar,* July 2, 1985.

"Al-Isra'iliyun Aktashafu Asliha fi Sayda Ightiyal Mas'ul fi 'Al-Haras al-Watani Tatawwur Ishtibak fi 'Ain al-Halwah" ('The Israelis Discovered Weapons in Sayda, The Assassination of an Official in the 'Home Guards,' Clash Developing in Ayn al-Halwa"), *al-Nahar,* May 5, 1984.

"Al-Mas'ul 'an al-Haras fi Haruf: La 'Alaqa Li bi-Ightiyal Harb" ('The Official for the Guards in Haruf: I Have No Tie to Harb's Assassination'), *al-Nahar,* April 12, 1984.

Alexander, Martin S., and J.F.V. Keiger, "France and the Algerian War: Strategy, Operations and Diplomacy," *Journal of Strategic Studies*, Vol. 25, No. 2, 2002, pp. 1–32.

Allam, Hannah, "Fallujah's Real Boss: Omar the Electrician," Knight-Ridder Newspapers, November 22, 2004.

Allen, Calvin H., Jr., "A Separate Place," *The Wilson Quarterly*, Vol. 11, No. 1, 1987.

Allès, Jean-François, *Commandos de chasse Gendarmerie: Algérie, 1959–1962, récit et témoignages*, Saint-Cloud: Atlante, 2000.

Anderson, John Ward, "U.S. Widens Offensive in Far Western Iraq," *Washington Post*, November 15, 2005.

". . . and Its Crumbling Militia," *Jane's Intelligence Weekly*, September 24, 1998.

Andrew, Christopher, and Vasili Mitrokhin, *The World Was Going Our Way: The KGB and the Battle for the Third World,* New York: Basic Books, 2005.

AQI Situation Report, declassified, translated internal AQI document, undated. As of July 5, 2012:
http://www.ctc.usma.edu/wp-content/uploads/2010/08/IZ-060316-01-Trans.pdf

Armstrong, Matthew C., "A Friend in the Desert," *Winchester Star*, April 8, 2008.

"Baghdad Hotel Bombing Kills Anti-Qaeda Sunni Sheikhs," *International Herald Tribune*, June 24, 2007.

Barak, Oren, and Gabriel Sheffer, "Israel's 'Security Network' and Its Impact: An Exploration of a New Approach," *International Journal of Middle East Studies*, Vol. 38, 2006.

Barboteu, Lieutenant Colonel (Auxiliary Forces Inspector), *Fiche à l'attention du Colonel Commandant la Zone Centre*, December 12, 1952, French Army Archives (Service historique de l'armée de terre) 10H 2158.

Barfield, Thomas, *Afghanistan: A Cultural and Political History*, Princeton, N.J.: Princeton University Press, 2010.

Bavly, Dan, and Eliahu Salpeter, *Fire in Beirut*, New York: Stein and Day, 1984.

Bergman, Ronen, "Fighting Blind," *Haaretz*, May 14, 1999a.

———, "Thanks for your Cooperation," *Haaretz*, October 29, 1999b.

Beydoun, Ahmad, "The South Lebanon Border Zone: A Local Perspective," *Journal of Palestine Studies*, Vol. 21, No. 3, Spring 1992.

Bird, Christiane, *The Sultan's Shadow: One Family's Rule at the Crossroads of East and West*, New York: Random House, 2010.

Black, Ian, and Benny Morris, *Israel's Secret Wars: A History of Israel's Intelligence Services*, New York: Grove Press, 1991.

Blanche, Ed, "Bizarre Yet Bloody Conflict Drags on in South Lebanon," *Jane's Intelligence Review*, Part One, September 1997, pp. 411–415.

Blanford, Nicholas, "New Reality for Lebanon," *Jane's Defence Weekly*, May 31, 2000.

———, *Warriors of God: Inside Hezbollah's Thirty-Year Struggle Against Israel*, New York: Random House, 2011.

BDM International, *Oral History of the Conflict in El Salvador, 1979–Present*, 6 vols., 1988. Available at the U.S. Army Military History Institute.

Bodin, Michel, *La France et ses soldats, Indochine, 1945–1954*, Paris: L'Harmattan, 1996.

———, *Dictionnaire de la guerre d'Indochine (1945–1954)*, Paris: Economica, 2004.

Boone, Jon, "US Keeps Secret Anti-Taliban Militia on a Bright Leash," *The Guardian*, March 8, 2010. As of November 2011:
http://www.guardian.co.uk/world/2010/mar/08/us-afghanistan-local-defence-militia

Bosch, Brian J., *The Salvadoran Officer Corps and the Final Offensive of 1981*, Jefferson, N.C.: McFarland & Co., 1999.

Braithwaite, Roderic, *Afgantsy: The Russians in Afghanistan, 1979–89*, London: Profile Books, 2011.

Brett, Gérard, *La tragédie des supplétifs: la fin des combats, quartier du Phu Duc–Tonkin 1953–1954*, Paris: L'Harmattan, 1998.

Brewington, Brooks R., "Combined Action Platoons: A Strategy for Peace Enforcement," Marine Command and Staff College thesis, 1996.

Bruno, Greg, "Meese: Bottom-Up Reconciliation in Iraq," *Council on Foreign Relations/Podcast*, interview with Col. Michael J. Meese, September 7, 2007. As of November 2011:
http://www.cfr.org/iraq/meese-bottom-up-reconciliation-iraq/p14157

Brynen, Rex, *Sanctuary and Survival: The PLO in Lebanon*, Boulder, Colo.: Westview Press, 1990.

Byman, Daniel, *A High Price: The Triumphs and Failures of Israeli Counterterrorism*, New York: Oxford University Press, 2011.

Byrne, Hugh, *El Salvador's Civil War: A Study of Revolution*, Boulder, Colo.: Lynne Rienner Publishers, 1996.

Cambanis, Thanassis, *A Privilege to Die: Inside Hezbollah's Legions and Their Endless War Against Israel*, Free Press, 2010.

Carter, Chelsea J., "General: Iraq Must Be Fair to Sons of Iraq," Associated Press, December 26, 2009.

Cassidy, Robert, "The Long Small War: Indigenous Forces for Counter-insurgency," *Parameters*, Summer 2006, pp. 47–62.

Challe, General Maurice, Directive No. 1 of December 22, foreword to the "Instruction pour la pacification en Algérie," document of December 10, 1959 (author's translation). French Army Archives (Service historique de l'armée de terre) 1H 1268/1.

———, "Directive concernant la politique à suivre en 1960 vis-à-vis des Musulmans combattant dans nos rangs," December 1959, French Army Archives (Service historique de l'armée de terre) 1H 1391/1.

Chandrasekaran, Rajiv, "U.S. Training Afghan Villagers to Fight the Taliban," *Washington Post*, April 27, 2010.

Chauvin, Stephanie, "Des appelés pas comme les autreses conscrits 'Français de souche nord-africains' pendant la guerre d'Algérie," *Vingtième Siècle. Revue d'histoire*, No. 48, October–December 1995, pp. 21–30.

Chayes, Sarah, "A Mullah Dies, and War Comes Knocking," *Washington Post*, November 18, 2007.

Checchi and Company Consulting, Inc., "Evaluation of the Social Stabilization and Municipal Development Strengthening Project," Report to USAID, June 1994.

Coban, Helena, *The Palestinian Liberation Organization: People, Power, and Politics*, New York: Cambridge University Press, 1984.

Cogny, General René, *Note de service, objet: Emploi des Compagnies de Supplétifs dans les Bataillons Mobiles F.T.E.O.*, January 12, 1954, French Army Archives (Service historique de l'armée de terre) 10H 2704.

―――――, *Note de service, objet: recrutement des supplétifs parmis les anciens ralliés V.M.*, Hanoi, November 7, 1953, French Army Archives (Service historique de l'armée de terre) 10H 2703.

―――――, *Note de service, objet: résorption des forces supplétives*, Haiphong, September 27, 1954, French Army Archives (Service historique de l'armée de terre) 10H 2703.

―――――, *Pour exécution*, Hanoi, July 19, 1953, French Army Archives (Service historique de l'armée de terre) 10H 2703.

Cohen, William B., "Legacy of Empire: The Algerian Connection," *Journal of Contemporary History*, Vol. 15, No. 1, January 1980, pp. 97–123.

Colby, William, with James McCargar, *Lost Victory: A Firsthand Account of America's Sixteen-Year Involvement in Vietnam*, Chicago: Contemporary Books, 1989.

Coll, Steve, "Afghan Rebel Faction Decries Attack by Rivals," *Washington Post*, July 20, 1989.

―――――, "Waning Support, Crippling Rifts Are Afghan Rebels' Other Foes," *Washington Post*, August 5, 1990.

―――――, *Ghost Wars: The Secret History of the CIA, Afghanistan, and bin Laden: From the Soviet Invasion to September 10, 2001*, New York: Penguin, 2004.

Coll, Steve, and William Branigin, "Afghanistan's Capital Falls to Muslim Rebels," *Washington Post*, April 26, 1992.

Combined Joint Special Operations Task Force Afghanistan (CJSOTF-A), press release, "Afghan National Police and Afghan Local Police Conduct Operation in Chashmak Village," July 11, 2011.

Commandement supérieur interarmées, 10e Région militaire, Etat-Major, 3e Bureau, "Fiche sur l'auto-défense des fermes," Algiers, February 14, 1958, French Army Archives (Service historique de l'armée de terre) 1H 1268/4.

Commander-in-Chief in Algeria, "Directive concernant la politique à suivre en 1960 vis-à-vis des Musulmans combattant dans nos rangs," December 1959, French Army Archives (Service historique de l'armée de terre) 1H 1391/1.

Convention passée entre le Commandant de la Zone Ouest de Pacification, et Monsieur Than Van Soai, Chef des Forces Armées Hoa-Hao, fixant la participation des Hoa-Hao à l'action de Pacification, Articles II and V, Cantho, May 18, 1947, French Army Archives (Service historique de l'armée de terre) 10H 995.

Couch, Dick, *The Sheriff of Ramadi: Navy SEALs and the Winning of al-Anbar,* Annapolis, Md.: Naval Institute Press, 2008.

Crain, Charles, "Iraq's New Job Insecurity," *Time/World*, Baghdad, December 24, 2007.

Cronin, Richard, "Afghanistan in 1988: Year of Decision," *Asian Survey*, Vol. 29, No. 2, February 1989.

Dagher, Sam, "How Fragile is Baghdad's Calm?" *Christian Science Monitor*, November 27, 2007.

―――, "Tribal Rivalries Persist as Iraqis Seek Local Posts," *New York Times*, January 19, 2009.

Dalloz, Jacques, *Dictionnaire de la guerre d'Indochine 1945–1954*, Paris: Armand Colin, 2006.

David, Michel, "Les maquis autochtones: une réponse à l'action politico-militaire Viêt-minh," in Maurice Vaïsse, ed., *L'Armée française dans la guerre d'Indochine (1946–1954): Adaptation ou inadaptation?* Brussels: Complexe, 2000, pp. 151–166.

―――, *Guerre secrète en Indochine: Les maquis autochtones face au Viêt-Minh, 1950–1955*, Paris: Lavauzelle, 2002.

Defense Intelligence Agency (DIA), "Guatemala and El Salvador: Civil Defense as a Counterinsurgency Tactic," November 1987 (declassified).

de Latour, Brigadier-General Pierre Boyer, *Instruction sur le fonctionnement des forces supplétives pour l'année 1949*, January 3, 1949.

―――, *Note de service,* July 5, 1949, French Army Archives (Service historique de l'armée de terre) 10H 2151.

de Linares, General Gonzales, *Note de service, objet: recrutement des supplétifs militaires*, Hanoi, August 3, 1951, French Army Archives (Service historique de l'armée de terre) 10H 2703.

―――, *Note de service, objet: supplétifs*, Hanoi, September 27, 1952, French Army Archives (Service historique de l'armée de terre) 10H 2703.

―――, *Note de service, objet: mesures de sécurité dans les unités de supplétifs*, Hanoi, May 13, 1953, French Army Archives (Service historique de l'armée de terre) 10H 2703.

Devlin, Peter, "State of the Insurgency in al-Anbar," III Marine Expeditionary Force G2 intelligence assessment report, August 17, 2006, in "Marine Corps Assessment of Iraq Situation," *Washington Post*, February 2, 2007. As of November 2011:
http://www.washingtonpost.com/wp-dyn/content/article/2007/02/02/AR2007020201197.html

Dockrill, Saki, *Britain's Retreat from East of Suez: The Choice Between Europe and the World*, London: Palgrave-MacMillan, 2002.

Dodge, Toby, "Iraq's Future: The Aftermath of Regime Change," *Adelphi Paper*, No. 372, London: International Institute for Strategic Studies, 2005.

Dorronsoro, Gilles, *Revolution Unending: Afghanistan, 1979 to the Present*, New York: Columbia University Press, 2005.

Duarte, Jose Napoleon, *Duarte: My Story*, New York: Putnam, 1986.

Dulac, Colonel André, *Note de service, objet: Organisation, entretien et emploi des Gardes Voies Ferrées*, Hanoi, January 13, 1952, French Army Archives (Service historique de l'armée de terre) 10H 2704.

Dumont, Marie, "Les unités territoriales," in Jean-Charles Jauffret and Maurice Vaïsse, eds., *Militaires et guérilla dans la guerre d'Algérie*, Brussels: Complexe, 2001, pp. 517–540.

Dunbar, Charles, "Afghanistan in 1986: The Balance Endures," *Asian Survey*, Vol. 27, No. 2, February 1987.

Edwards, David, *Before Taliban: Genealogies of the Afghan Jihad*, Berkeley, Calif.: University of California Press, 2002.

Eisenberg, Laurie Zittrain, "From Benign to Malign: Israeli-Lebanese Relations, 1948–1978," in Clive Jones and Sergio Catignani, eds., *Israel and Hizbollah: An Asymmetric Conflict in Historical and Comparative Perspective*, New York: Routledge, 2010.

Eliot, Theodore L., "Afghanistan in 1989: Stalemate," *Asian Survey*, Vol. 30, No. 2, February 1990.

———, "Afghanistan in 1990: Groping Towards Peace?" *Asian Survey*, Vol. 31, No. 2, February 1991.

Ely, General Paul, *Note de service, objet: résorption des forces supplétives*, September 20, 1954, French Army Archives (Service historique de l'armée de terre) 10H 2703.

État-major interarmées et des forces terrestres (EMIFT), *Fiche sur les forces supplétives*, February 23, 1953, French Army Archives (Service historique de l'armée de terre) 10H 1020.

Faivre, Maurice, *Un village de harkis: des Babors au pays drouais*, Paris: L'Harmattan, 1994.

———, *Les combattants musulmans de la guerre d'Algérie: des soldats sacrifiés*, Paris: L'Harmattan, 1995.

———, "L'histoire des Harkis," *Guerres mondiales et conflits contemporains*, No. 202–203, 2001, pp. 55–63.

Harvey, Tom, email response to interview questions, May 2011.

Hautreux, François-Xavier, "L'engagement des harkis (1954–1962). Essai de périodisation," *Vingtième Siècle. Revue d'histoire*, No. 90, April–June 2006, pp. 33–45.

———, "Les supplétifs pendant la guerre d'Algérie," in Fatima Besnaci-Lancou and Gilles Manceron, eds., *Les harkis dans la colonisation et ses suites*, Ivry-sur-Seine: Editions de l'Atelier, 2008, pp. 37–50.

Healy, Jack, "20 Police Officers Killed in Western Iraq," *New York Times*, March 5, 2012.

Heggoy, Alf Andrew, *Insurgency and Counterinsurgency in Algeria*, Bloomington, Ind.: Indiana University Press, 1972.

Helmer, Daniel Isaac, "Flipside of the COIN: Israel's Lebanese Incursion Between 1982–2000," *The Long War Series Occasional Paper 21*, Fort Leavenworth, Kan.: Combat Studies Institute Press, 2007.

Hemingway, Al, *Our War Was Different: Marine Combined Action Platoons in Vietnam*, Annapolis, Md.: Naval Institute Press, 1994.

Hennessy, Michael A., *Strategy in Vietnam: The Marines and Revolutionary Warfare in I Corps, 1965–1972*, Westport, Conn.: Praeger, 1997.

Herzog, Chaim, and Shlomo Gazit, *The Arab-Israeli Wars: War and Peace in the Middle East from the 1948 War of Independence to the Present,* 2nd ed., New York: Vintage Books, 2004.

Hickey, Gerald C., *Free in the Forest: Ethnohistory of the Vietnamese Central Highlands 1954–1976*, New Haven, Conn.: Yale University Press, 1982.

Hirst, David, "South Lebanon: The War That Never Ends?" *Journal of Palestine Studies*, Vol. 28, No. 3, Spring 1999, pp. 5–18.

Horne, Alistair, *A Savage War of Peace: Algeria 1954–1962*, New York: The Viking Press, 1978.

Hosmer, Stephen, and Sybille Crane, eds., *Counterinsurgency: A Symposium, April 16–20, 1962*, Santa Monica, Calif.: RAND Corporation, R-412-1, 1963, 2006. As of June 10, 2012:
http://www.rand.org/pubs/reports/R412-1.html

Hughes, Geraint, "A 'Model Campaign' Reappraised: The Counter-Insurgency War in Dhofar, Oman, 1965–1975," *Journal of Strategic Studies,* Vol. 32, No. 2, April 2009.

Human Rights Watch, "Torture in Khiam Prison: Responsibility and Accountability," October 27, 1999. As of November 2011:
http://www.hrw.org/news/1999/10/27/torture-khiam-prison-responsibility-and-accountability

Hunt, Richard, *Pacification: The American Struggle for Vietnam's Hearts and Minds,* Boulder, Colo.: Westview Press, 1995.

Hunter, Catherine, "Lebanon: The South Lebanon Army (SLA) and Child Recruitment: Putting the Pressure on Whom?" *Coalition to Stop the Use of Child Soldiers,* Forum on armed groups and the involvement of children in armed conflict, Chateau de Bossey, Switzerland, July 4–7, 2006.

"In Brief—Former SLA Militiamen Jailed," *Jane's Defense Weekly,* September 27, 2000.

Institut national de la statistique et des études économiques (INSEE), "Pyramide des âges au 1er janvier 1957, France métropolitaine, " INSEE website. As of April 2012:
http://www.insee.fr/fr/themes/detail.asp?ref_id=ir-sd2006&page=irweb/sd2006/dd/html/p1957.htm

Instruction provisoire sur le statut du partisan indochinois, Saigon, January 29, 1948, French Army Archives (Service historique de l'armée de terre) 10H 2703.

International Crisis Group, *Loose Ends: Iraq's Security Forces Between U.S. Drawdown and Withdrawal,* Brussels: Middle East Report No. 99, October 26, 2010.

"Iraqi Rebels Turn on Qaeda in Western City," Reuters, January 23, 2006.

Islamic Republic of Afghanistan Ministry of Interior, "ALP Adjusted Procedure," February 2011a.

———, "Afghan Local Police Fact Sheet," July 2011b.

Ives, Christopher, *U.S. Special Forces and Counterinsurgency in Vietnam: Military Innovation and Institutional Failure, 1961–1963,* New York: Routledge, 2007.

Jaber, Hala, *Hezbollah: Born with a Vengeance,* New York: Columbia University Press, 1997.

Jabir, Mundhir Mahmud, *Al-Sharit al-Lubnani al-Muhtall: Masalik al Ihtilal, Masarat al-Muwajaha, Masa'ir al-Ahali* (The Occupied Lebanese Border Strip: The Paths of Occupation, the Lines of Confrontation, and the Fate of the Population), Beirut: Institute for Palestine Studies, 1999.

Jaffe, Greg, "Tribal Connections: How Courting Sheiks Slowed Violence in Iraq," *Wall Street Journal,* August 8, 2007.

Jalali, Ali, and Lester Grau, *The Other Side of the Mountain: Mujahideen Tactics in the Soviet-Afghan War,* Quantico, Va.: Marine Corps Studies and Analysis, 1999.

"Jane's Intelligence Watch Report—Daily Update, 16 February 1999," Vol. 6, Issue 030, February 16, 1999. As of July 18, 2012: http://jtic.janes.com/Search/documentView.do?docId=/content1/janesdata/mags/ iwr/history/iwr1999/iv6n030b.htm@current&pageSelected=allJanes&keyword=D aily%20Update&backPath=http://jtic.janes.com/Search&Prod_Name=IWR&

Jauffret, Jean-Charles, "Une armée à deux vitesses en Algérie (1954–1962): Réserves générales et troupes de secteur," in Jean-Charles Jauffret and Maurice Vaïsse, eds., *Militaires et guérilla dans la guerre d'Algérie*, Brussels: Complexe, 2001, pp. 21–37.

Jeapes, Tony, *SAS Secret War: Operation Storm in the Middle East*, Mechanicsburg, Pa.: Stackpole Books, 2005.

Jones, Clive, "Israeli Counter-Insurgency Strategy and the War in South Lebanon 1985–97," *Small Wars and Insurgencies*, Vol. 8, No. 3, Winter 1997.

———, "'A Reach Greater Than the Grasp': Israeli Intelligence and the Conflict in South Lebanon 1990–2000," *Intelligence and National Security*, Vol. 16, No. 3, Autumn 2001.

Jones, Seth G., and Arturo Munoz, *Afghanistan's Local War: Building Local Defense Forces*, Santa Monica, Calif.: RAND Corporation, MG-1002-MCIA, 2010. As of June 10, 2012: http://www.rand.org/pubs/monographs/MG1002.html

Kalyvas, Stathis N., *The Logic of Violence in Civil War*, Cambridge: Cambridge University Press, 2006.

Kaplow, Larry, "Making a Lasting Peace with the Sunni Awakening Movement," *Newsweek* Baghdad Blog, May 19, 2009. As of November 2011: http://www.thedailybeast.com/newsweek/blogs/check-point-baghdad/2009/05/19/ making-a-lasting-peace-with-the-sunni-awakening-movement.html

Kaufman, Asher, "From the Litani to Beirut: Israel's Invasions," in Clive Jones and Sergio Catignani, eds., *Israel and Hizbollah: An Asymmetric Conflict in Historical and Comparative Perspective*, New York: Routledge, 2010.

Kelly, Francis J., *U.S. Army Special Forces 1961–1971*, Washington, D.C.: Center of Military History, 1973.

Khalidi, Rashid, "Under Siege: P.L.O Decisionmaking During the 1982 War," New York: Columbia University Press, 1986.

Khan, Rais, "Pakistan in 1991: Light and Shadows," *Asian Survey*, Vol. 32, No. 2, February 1992.

Komer, Robert W., *Organization and Management of the New Model Pacification Program: 1966–1969*, Santa Monica, Calif.: RAND Corporation, D-20104, 1970. As of June 10, 2012: http://www.rand.org/pubs/documents/D20104.html

Krause, Lincoln, "Playing for the Breaks: Insurgent Mistakes," *Parameters*, Autumn 2009, pp. 49–64. As of June 18, 2012:
https://www.hsdl.org/?search&exact=Krause%2C+Lincoln+B.&searchfield=creato
r&collection=limited&submitted=Search&so=date&creator=Krause%2C+Lincoln
+B.&fct&page=1

Krepinevich, Andrew, *The Army and Vietnam*, Baltimore, Md.: Johns Hopkins University Press, 1986.

Kukis, Mark, "Turning Iraq's Tribes Against Al-Qaeda," *Time*, December 26, 2006.

Kuperman, Alan, "The Stinger Missile and U.S. Intervention in Afghanistan," *Political Science Quarterly*, Vol. 114, No. 2, Summer 1999.

Lacoste, Robert, Minister of Algeria, letter on "Auto-défense des fermes," Algiers, July 6, 1957.

———, "Note sur la sécurité des SAS," Algiers, February 26, 1958, French Army Archives (Service historique de l'armée de terre) 1H 2556/1.

Ladwig, Walter C. III, "Supporting Allies in Counterinsurgency: Britain and the Dhofar Rebellion," *Small Wars and Insurgencies*, Vol. 19, No. 1, March 2008.

"Lahad Tafaqqad Mawaq' wa Zara al-Salahiya: Jayshna li-l-Muslim Kamma li-l-Musihi wa Satalmasun bi-Fadlihi al-Istiqrar Qariban" ("Lahad Inspected Positions and Visited Salahiya: Our Army Is for the Muslims as Well as the Christians, and You Will Notice Stability Thanks to It Soon"), *al-Nahar*, May 21, 1984.

Lavie, Aviv, "Never Never Land, On Khiam Prison in Southern Lebanon," *Middle East Report*, No. 203, Spring 1997.

Le Pautremat, Pascal, "Le commando Georges," *Guerres mondiales et conflits contemporains*, No. 213, 2004, pp. 95–103.

Lefèvre, Mathieu, *Local Defence in Afghanistan: A Review of Government-Backed Initiatives*, Afghan Analyst Network, Thematic Report, May 2010. As of November 2011:
http://aan-afghanistan.com/uploads/20100525MLefevre-LDIpaper.pdf

Leland, John, "Iraq Sentences Sunni Leader to Death," *New York Times*, November 19, 2009.

Lemattre, Bernard, "Étude comparée de la stratégie du Viêt minh et des stratégies françaises pendant la guerre d'Indochine," in Jean-Pierre Renaud and Jean-Luc Susini, eds., *Paix et guerre en Indochine 1945–1955*, Paris: Lavauzelle, 2002, pp. 49–78.

Lemond, Lt-Colonel, letter of January 29, 1959, on *Commandos de chasse*, author's translation, French Army Archives (Service historique de l'armée de terre) 1H 4184/1.

"Le Conseiller politique du gouvernement fédéral à monsieur le Général Commandant supérieur des T.F.E.O.," letter, Saigon, February 20, 1946, French Army Archives (Service historique de l'armée de terre) 10H 995.

Le partisan ne doit plus être un soldat au rabais, in Lieutenant Colonel Cazalaa citing General Charles Chanson, *Fiche, Objet: Statut du Partisan,* Saigon, June 17, 1948, French Army Archives (Service historique de l'armée de terre) 10H 995.

Logevall, Fredrik, *Choosing War: The Lost Chance for Peace and the Escalation of War in Vietnam,* Berkeley, Calif.: University of California Press, 2001.

Long, Austin, *On "Other War": Lessons from Five Decades of RAND Counterinsurgency Research,* Santa Monica, Calif.: RAND Corporation, MG-482-OSD, 2006. As of June 10, 2012:
http://www.rand.org/pubs/monographs/MG482.html

———, "The Anbar Awakening," *Survival,* Vol. 50, No. 2, March/April 2008.

———, "First War Syndrome: Military Culture, Professionalization, and Counterinsurgency," dissertation, Massachusetts Institute of Technology, 2010.

Lyakhovskiy, Aleksandr, "Inside the Soviet Invasion of Afghanistan and the Seizure of Kabul, December 1979," Cold War International History Project Working Paper No. 51, January 2007.

Lyall, Jason, "Are Coethnics More Effective Counterinsurgents? Evidence from the Second Chechen War," *American Political Science Review,* Vol. 104, No. 1, February 2010.

Lynch, Marc, "Explaining the Awakening: Engagement, Publicity, and the Transformation of Iraqi Sunni Political Attitudes," *Security Studies,* Vol. 20, No. 1, March 2011.

Maazouzi, Djemaa, "H comme harki, honte, honneur: nom du traître et traîtres mots," *Post-Scriptum.ORG,* No. 10, Fall 2009. As of September 23, 2011:
http://www.post-scriptum.org/alpha/a ticles/2009_10_maazouzi.pdf

Madden, Dan, "A History of Village Stability Operations and the Afghan Local Police," April 2011 (unpublished manuscript).

Mahieu, Alban, "Les effectifs de l'armée française en Algérie (1954–1962)," in Jean-Charles Jauffret and Maurice Vaïsse, eds., *Militaires et guérilla dans la guerre d'Algérie,* Brussels: Complexe, 2001, pp. 21–37.

Malkasian, Carter, "Signaling Resolve, Democratization, and the First Battle of Fallujah," *Journal of Strategic Studies,* Vol. 29, No. 3, June 2006.

———, "A Thin Blue Line in the Sand," *Democracy,* No. 5, Summer 2007a.

———, "Did the Coalition Need More Forces in Iraq?" *Joint Forces Quarterly,* No. 46, Summer 2007b.

Malraison, Captain, *Objet: creation d'une auto-défense à Tien-My*, October 19, 1952, French Army Archives (Service historique de l'armée de terre) 10H 2158.

Manning, Stephen, "CIA Chief: Military Strikes Offer Lessons," Associated Press, September 17, 2008.

Manwaring, Max, and Court Prisk, eds., *El Salvador at War: An Oral History of the Conflict from the 1979 Insurrection to the Present*, Washington, D.C.: National Defense University Press, 1988.

Margueron, Chef de bataillon, *"Rapport sur les partisans,"* May 2, 1946, French Army Archives (Service historique de l'armée de terre) 10H 995.

Marquis, Jefferson, "The Other Warriors: American Social Science and Nation Building in Vietnam," *Diplomatic History*, Vol. 24, No. 1, 2000.

Marten, Kim, *Warlords: Strong-Arm Brokers in Weak States,* Ithaca, N.Y.: Cornell University Press, 2012.

Mathias, Grégor, *Les sections administratives spécialisées en Algérie: entre idéal et réalité, 1955–1962*, Paris: L'Harmattan, 1998.

Matthews, Matt, "Operation AL FAJR: A Study in Army and Marine Corps Joint Operations," *Long War Occasional Paper 20*, Ft. Leavenworth, Kan.: Combat Studies Institute Press, 2006.

McCary, John A. "The Anbar Awakening: An Alliance of Incentives," *The Washington Quarterly*, Vol. 32, No. 1, January 2009.

McManus, Doyle, "U.S. and Soviets Will Halt Afghan Arms Aid by Jan. 1," *Los Angeles Times*, September 14, 1991.

McWilliams, Timothy S., and Kurtis P. Wheeler, eds., *Al-Anbar Awakening: U.S. Marines and Counterinsurgency in Iraq, 2004–2009*, Volume I, *American Perspective*, Quantico, Va.: Marine Corps University Press, 2009.

"Middle East, South Lebanon Army—A Profile," *Jane's Intelligence Review*, May 1, 2000.

Minister of Algeria, letter on *Objet: Auto-défense des exploitations agricoles*, December 12, 1957, French Army Archives (Service historique de l'armée de terre) 1H 1105/2.

Monneret, Jean, *La phase finale de la guerre d'Algérie*, Paris: L'Harmattan, 2000.

Moore, Scott W., *Gold, Not Purple: Lessons from USAID-MILGP Cooperation in El Salvador, 1980–1992*, thesis, Naval Post-Graduate School, 1997. As of June 13, 2012:
http://www.dtic.mil/cgi-bin/GetTRDoc?AD=ADA341399

Morel, Lieutenant Colonel, commanding the Hocmon sector, *Note de service, objet: Partisans*, April 23, 1949, French Army Archives (Service historique de l'armée de terre) 10H 2151.

Morin, Monte "Who's Your Enemy?" *Stars and Stripes*, June 3, 2007.

Mowles, Chris, "The Israeli Occupation of South Lebanon," *Third World Quarterly*, Vol. 8, No. 4, October 1986.

Muelle, Raymond, *Commandos et maquis: service action en Indochine, GCMA Tonkin 1951–1954*, Paris: Presses de la Cité, 1993.

"Muhawalatayn li-Ightiyal Mas'ulin fi 'al-Haras' Qadhifa 'Ala Mawq' Jal al-Bahr wa 'Ubuwa 'ala Dawriya fi Tayr Dabba" ("Two Attempts to Assassinate Officials in the 'Guards': A Mortar on the Jal Bahr Position and an Explosive on a Patrol in Tayr Dabba"), *al-Nahar*, June 11, 1984.

Mulrine, Anne, "What's Behind the Latest Sunni-Shiite Clashes in Iraq," *U.S. News and World Report*, March 31, 2009.

Multi-National Force–Iraq, "Tearing Down al-Qaida in Iraq," press briefing, December 2006.

———, "Sunni, Shia Sheikhs Present United Front Against al-Qaeda," Press Release, November 10, 2007.

"Najibullah's Poker Game," *The Economist*, March 14, 1992.

National Security Action Memorandum 328, Presidential Decisions RE U.S. Policy in Vietnam, April 6, 1965, in *The Pentagon Papers*, Gravel Edition, Vol. 3, pp. 702–703.

NATO Training Mission–Afghanistan, "Afghanistan Local Police Update" (unclassified briefing), August 4, 2011.

Navarre, General Henri, *Note de service, objet: recrutement du G.C.M.A.*, Saigon, October 29, 1953, French Army Archives (Service historique de l'armée de terre) 10H 2375.

Naylor, Sean D., "No Easy Task: Making the Afghan Special Forces," *ArmyTimes*, May 18, 2010. As of November 2011:
http://www.armytimes.com/news/2010/05/army_afghan_special_forces_051810w/

Nickmeyer, Ellen, and Jonathan Finer, "Insurgents Assert Control over Town Near Syrian Border," *Washington Post*, September 6, 2005.

"Nisbat Tatawwu' fi 'al-Jaysh al-Janubi' Ila Irtifa'" (Volunteer Rate in the 'South Army' Rising), *al-Nahar*, April 17, 1984.

Nordland, Rod, and Alissa Rubin, "Sunni Militiamen Say Iraq Didn't Keep Job Promises," *New York Times*, March 23, 2009.

Norton, Augustus Richard, *Hezbollah: A Short History*, New York: Princeton University Press, 2007.

———, "Hizbollah and the Israeli Withdrawal from Southern Lebanon," *Journal of Palestine Studies*, Vol. 30, No. 1, Autumn 2000.

Norton, Augustus Richard, and Jillian Schwedler, "(In) Security Zones in South Lebanon," *Journal of Palestine Studies*, Vol. 23, No. 1, Autumn 1993.

Notice sur l'organisation générale des forces armées des États associés, forces des minorités ethniques, forces para-militaires, November 25, 1949, French Army Archives (Service historique de l'armée de terre) 10H 239.

Office of the Special Inspector General for Iraq Reconstruction, *Sons of Iraq Program: Results Are Uncertain and Financial Controls Were Weak*, January 2011. Audit Report 11-010. As of June 18, 2012:
http://www.sigir.mil/directorates/audits/auditReports.html

Oliker, Olga, *Building Afghanistan's Security Forces in Wartime: The Soviet Experience,* Santa Monica, Calif.: RAND Corporation, MG-1078-A, 2011. As of June 14, 2012:
http://www.rand.org/pubs/monographs/MG1078.html

Olsen, Tiraporn, "Maj. Gen. John Johnson Aug 27," *Operation New Dawn,* Official Website of United States Forces–Iraq, transcript for DoD News Briefing from Iraq, August 27, 2009. As of November 2011:
http://www.usf-iraq.com/?option=com_content&task=view&id=27736&Itemid=131

O'Shea, Brendan, "Israel's Vietnam?" *Studies in Conflict and Terrorism*, Ireland: University College, Vol. 3, No. 3, 1998.

"Operational Report—Lessons Learned, Headquarters, Americal Division Artillery, Period Ending 31 January 1970," April 21, 1970. As of June 12, 2012:
http://www.dtic.mil/dtic/tr/fulltext/u2/508726.pdf

Operations of U.S. Marine Forces, Vietnam, April 1966, Folder 001, US Marine Corps History Division Vietnam War Documents Collection, The Vietnam Center and Archive, Texas Tech University.

———, May 1966, Folder 001, US Marine Corps History Division Vietnam War Documents Collection, The Vietnam Center and Archive, Texas Tech University.

———, June 1966, Folder 001, US Marine Corps History Division Vietnam War Documents Collection, The Vietnam Center and Archive, Texas Tech University.

———, September 1966, Folder 001, US Marine Corps History Division Vietnam War Documents Collection, The Vietnam Center and Archive, Texas Tech University.

———, September 1969, Folder 001, US Marine Corps History Division Vietnam War Documents Collection, The Vietnam Center and Archive, Texas Tech University.

Pentagon Papers, Gravel Edition, Vol. 3, April 6, 1965.

Perry, Tony, "Tea and Tribal Conflict in Iraq," *Los Angeles Times*, January 22, 2008.

Petersen, Roger, *Resistance and Rebellion: Lessons from Eastern Europe*, New York: Cambridge University Press, 2001.

Petersen, Scott, "The Rise and Fall of Ansar al-Islam," *Christian Science Monitor*, October 16, 2003.

Peterson, J. E., "Oman's Diverse Society: Southern Oman," *Middle East Journal*, Vol. 58, No. 2, Spring 2004.

———, *Oman's Insurgencies: The Sultanate's Struggle for Supremacy*, London: Saqi Books, 2007.

Peterson, Michael E., *Combined Action Platoons: The U.S. Marines' Other War in Vietnam*, Westport, Conn.: Praeger Press, 1989.

Petraeus, David, "Report to Congress on the Situation in Iraq," Senate Armed Services Committee, April 8–9, 2008.

Phares, Walid, "Liberating Lebanon," *Middle East Quarterly*, December 1996.

Pimlott, John, "The French Army: from Indochina to Chad, 1946–1984," in Ian F. W. Beckett and John Pimlott, eds., *Armed Forces and Modern Counter-Insurgency*, New York: St Martin's Press, 1985.

Pottier, Philippe, "GCMA/GMI: A French Experience in Counterinsurgency During the French Indochina War," *Small Wars & Insurgencies*, Vol. 16, No. 2, 2005, pp. 125–146.

Prados, John, *Lost Crusader: The Secret Wars of CIA Director William Colby*, Oxford, UK: Oxford University Press, 2003.

Pressfield, Steven, "The Full Document at Last!" Steven Pressfield Online/AGORA, October 29, 2009. As of November 2011: http://www.stevenpressfield.com/2009/10/one-tribe-at-a-time-4-the-full-document-at-last/

Raghavan, Sudarsan, "In Fallujah, Peace Through Brute Strength," *Washington Post*, March 24, 2008.

Rapport du Lt-Colonel Carbonel, commandant le secteur de Cao-Bang *Sur la désertion de la section de partisans pionniers No. 1 dans la nuit du 12 au 13 juin 1948*, French Army Archives (Service historique de l'armée de terre) 10H 995.

Rashid, Ahmed, "Friendless Foe," *Far Eastern Economic Review*, October 25, 1990.

"Rebel Cabinet Holds 1st Session in Afghanistan," *Los Angeles Times*, March 11, 1989.

Redon, Colonel, commanding the Western area, Letter: *Extraits concernant les forces supplétives*, February 23, 1949, French Army Archives (Service historique de l'armée de terre) 10H 2151.

Rid, Thomas, "The Nineteenth Century Origins of Counterinsurgency Doctrine," *Journal of Strategic Studies*, Vol. 33, No. 5, 2010, pp. 727–758.

Roy, Olivier, *Islam and Resistance in Afghanistan,* Cambridge, UK: Cambridge University Press, 1986.

Rubin, Alissa, "Sheik's Allies Vow Revenge for His Killing," *New York Times*, September 15, 2007.

Rubin, Barnett, "Afghanistan in 1993: Abandoned but Surviving," *Asian Survey*, Vol. 34, No. 2, February 1994.

Rupert, James, "Afghanistan Rebels Lose Key Battle," *Washington Post*, July 8, 1989.

Russell, James A., *Innovation, Transformation, and War: Counterinsurgency Operations in Anbar and Ninewa Provinces, 2005–2007,* Stanford, Calif.: Stanford University Press, 2011.

Salan, General Raoul, *Note de service, Objet: Organisation des forces supplétives F.T.E.O. du Nord Viet-Nam*, Saigon, September 27, 1951, French Army Archives (Service historique de l'armée de terre) 10H 2703.

Sayigh, Yezid, *Armed Struggle and the Search for State: The Palestinian National Movement 1949–1993*, New York: Oxford University Press, 1997.

Scarborough, Rowan, "Afghan Local Police Key to Success Against Taliban," *Washington Times*, March 29, 2012.

Schwarz, Benjamin, *American Counterinsurgency Doctrine and El Salvador: The Frustrations of Reform and the Illusions of Nation Building*, Santa Monica, Calif.: RAND Corporation, R-4042-USDP, 1991. As of June 12, 2012: http://www.rand.org/pubs/reports/R4042.html

Searle, Thomas R., "Tribal Engagement in Al Anbar Province: The Critical Role of Special Operations Forces," *Joint Forces Quarterly*, No. 50, Summer 2008.

Sela, Avraham, "Civil Society, the Military, and National Security: The Case of Israel's Security Zone in South Lebanon," *Israel Studies*, Vol. 12, No. 1, Spring 2007.

Shafer, D. Michael, *Deadly Paradigms: The Failure of U.S. Counterinsurgency Policy*, Princeton, N.J.: Princeton University Press, 1988.

Shulimson, Jack, Leonard A. Blasiol, Charles R. Smith, and David A. Dawson, *U.S. Marines in Vietnam: The Defining Year 1968,* Washington, D.C.: United States Marine Corps, History and Museums Division, 1997.

Shulimson, Jack, and Charles Johnson, *U.S. Marines In Vietnam: The Landing and the Buildup 1965,* Washington, D.C.: United States Marine Corps History and Museums Division, 1978.

Sobelman, Daniel, "Israel Expels 25 Relatives of SLA Defectors to Lebanon," *Haaretz*, April 8, 1999.

———, "Hezbollah's 'Execution' of SLA Man Signals a New Policy," *Haaretz*, March 23, 2000.

———, "Hizbollah—from Terror to Resistance, Towards a National Defence Strategy," in Clive Jones and Sergio Catignani, eds., *Israel and Hizbollah: An Asymmetric Conflict in Historical and Comparative Perspective,* New York: Routledge, 2010.

Stanton, Shelby, *Green Berets at War: U.S. Army Special Forces in Southeast Asia 1956–1975*, New York: Dell, 1985.

Stachura, Christopher, "Afghan Leaders, U.S. Soldiers Initiate Public Protection Program," U.S. Department of Defense, Wardak Province, Afghanistan, May 13, 2009. As of November 2011:
http://www.defense.gov/news/newsarticle.aspx?id=54332

Syndicate of plantation owners, "Letter to the military commandment in South Vietnam," September 19, 1949, French Army Archives (Service historique de l'armée de terre) 10H 2151.

Sussman, Tina, "Slain Sheik a Stark Contrast to His Brother," *Los Angeles Times*, October 13, 2007.

Taber, Robert, *War of the Flea: The Classic Study of Guerrilla Warfare*, New York: Potomac Books, 2002 (original edition, 1965).

"Tahqiq li-Reuters min al-Mantaqa al-Hadudiya: 38 Wahda min al-Haras al-Watani wa Isra'il Da'iman fi-l-Sura" ("A Reuters Investigation in the Border Region: 38 Home Guards Units and Israel Is Always in the Picture"), *al-Nahar*, May 13, 1985.

Tarzi, Shah, "Politics of the Afghan Resistance Movement: Cleavages, Disunity and Fragmentation," *Asian Survey*, Vol. 31, No. 6, June 1991.

——— ,"Afghanistan in 1991: A Glimmer of Hope," *Asian Survey*, Vol. 32, No. 2, February 1992.

———, "Afghanistan in 1992: A Hobbesian State of Nature," *Asian Survey*, Vol. 33, No. 2, February 1993.

"Tawatyur Bayn al-Irlandiyin wa-l-Isra'iliyin wa Iqbal 'ala Tatawwu' fi 'al-Haras'" ("Tension between the Irish and Israelis, and Concern Over Volunteering in the Guards"), *al-Nahar,* May 24, 1984.

Tefft, Sheila, "As Arms Supply Winds Down, Afghan Rebels Close Ranks," *Christian Science Monitor,* November 15, 1990.

Teulières, André, *L'Indochine, guerres et paix,* Paris: Lavauzelle, 1985.

Tourret, Hubert, "L'évolution de la tactique du corps expéditionnaire français en Extrême-Orient," in Maurice Vaïsse, ed., *L'Armée française dans la guerre d'Indochine (1946-1954): Adaptation ou inadaptation?* Brussels: Complexe, 2000, pp. 173–187.

Tsantarliotis, Achilles, "Karmah Sheikhs Committed to Progression," October 4, 2008. As of June 14, 2012:
http://www.marines.mil/unit/1stmardiv/1stregiment/rct1/Pages/ Karmahsheikscommittedtoprogression.aspx

"Two Locals Headed Fallujah Insurgency," Associated Press, November 24, 2004.

Tyson, Ann Scott, "In a Volatile Region of Iraq, US Military Takes Two Paths," *Washington Post,* September 15, 2006.

———, "A Deadly Clash at Donkey Island," *Washington Post,* August 19, 2007.

U.S. Central Command Afghanistan–Pakistan Center, "*Local Defense Forces in Afghanistan: Historical Context and Best Practices,*" March 2011.

U.S. Central Intelligence Agency (CIA), "El Salvador: Government and Insurgent Prospects," Washington, D.C.: National Security Archive, George Washington University, 1989.

U.S. Marine Corps History staff interview, Staff Brigadier General Nuri al-Din al-Fahadawi, in Gary Montgomery and Timothy McWilliams, eds., *Al-Anbar Awakening,* Volume II: *Iraqi Perspectives,* Quantico, Va.: Marine Corps University, 2009.

Urban, Mark, *Task Force Black,* New York: Little, Brown, 2010.

Venter, Al, "South Lebanese Army Combats Internal Disintegration," *Jane's International Defense Review,* August 1996.

Waghelstein, John, "Ruminations of a Pachyderm or What I Learned in the Counter-insurgency Business," *Small Wars and Insurgencies,* Vol. 5, No. 3, 1994.

Walker, U.S. Ambassador William, cable to Secretary of State James Baker, October 1990, declassified.

Weaver, Timothy, "Afghan Guerilla Assault on Jalalabad Stalls," *Washington Post,* March 26, 1989.

Wehrey, Frederic, "A Clash of Wills: Hizballah's Psychological Campaign Against Israel in South Lebanon," *Small Wars and Insurgencies,* Vol. 13, No. 2, Autumn 2002, pp. 53–74.

West Jr., F. J. "Bing," *The Village,* rev. ed., New York: Simon and Schuster, 2003.

————, *No True Glory: A Frontline Account of the Battle for Fallujah,* New York: Bantam, 2005.

Westad, Odd Arne, "Concerning the Situation in 'A': New Russian Evidence on the Soviet Intervention in Afghanistan," *Cold War International History Project Bulletin* 8–9, Winter 1996/1997.

Weymouth, Lally, "An Afghan Rebel Chief Tells America 'No Deal,'" *Washington Post,* September 17, 1989.

Woerner, Frederick, *Report of the El Salvador Military Strategy Assistance Team,* November 1981. As of June 13, 2012:
http://www.dod.mil/pubs/foi/International_security_affairs/latinAmerica/460.pdf

Woodward, Bob, *The War Within: A Secret White House History 2006–2008,* New York: Simon and Schuster, 2008.

Yaniv, Avner, *Dilemmas of Security: Politics, Strategy, and the Israeli Experience in Lebanon,* New York: Oxford University Press, 1987.

Zimmerman, Rebecca, Alton Buland, Todd Helmus, and Bryce Loidolt, *"If You've Seen One VSP, You've Seen One VSP,"* CFSOCC-A Commander's Initiatives Group, September, 2010.

Ziring, Lawrence, "Pakistan in 1989: The Politics of Stalemate," *Asian Survey,* Vol. 30, No. 2, February 1990.

————, "Pakistan in 1990: The Fall of Benazir Bhutto," *Asian Survey,* Vol. 31, No. 2, February 1991.